Meditations

on the Supper of our Lord, and the Hours of the Passion.

BERLIN: ASHER & CO., 53 MOHRENSTRASSE.
NEW YORK: C. SCRIBNER & CO.; LEYPOLDT & HOLT.
PHILADELPHIA: J. B. LIPPINCOTT & CO.

Meditations

on the Supper of our Lord, and the Hours of the Passion,

by

Cardinal John Bonaventura

the Seraphic Doctor.

Drawn into English Verse by Robert Manning of Brunne.

(ABOUT 1315—1330.)

EDITED FROM THE MSS. IN THE BRITISH MUSEUM AND
THE BODLEIAN LIBRARY, OXFORD,

with Introduction and Glossary

BY

J. MEADOWS COWPER, F.R.H.S.,

EDITOR OF 'THE TIMES' WHISTLE,' 'ENGLAND IN HENRY VIII'S TIME,' 'THE SELECT
WORKS OF ARCHDEACON CROWLEY,' ETC. ETC.

LONDON:
PUBLISHED FOR THE EARLY ENGLISH TEXT SOCIETY,
BY N. TRÜBNER & CO., 57 & 59, LUDGATE HILL.

OXFORD
UNIVERSITY PRESS

Great Clarendon Street, Oxford OX2 6DP
United Kingdom

Oxford University Press is a department of the University of Oxford.
It furthers the University's objective of excellence in research, scholarship,
and education by publishing worldwide. Oxford is a registered trade mark of
Oxford University Press in the UK and in certain other countries

© The Early English Text Society 1875

The moral rights of the authors have been asserted

Database right Oxford University Press (maker)

First Edition published in 1875
Reprinted 1924, 1997

All rights reserved. No part of this publication may be reproduced,
stored in a retrieval system, or transmitted, in any form or by any means,
without the prior permission in writing of Oxford University Press,
or as expressly permitted by law, or under terms agreed with the appropriate
reprographics rights organization. Enquiries concerning reproduction
outside the scope of the above should be sent to the Rights Department,
Oxford University Press, at the address above

You must not circulate this book in any other form
and you must impose this same condition on any acquirer

Published in the United States of America by Oxford University Press
198 Madison Avenue, New York, NY 10016, United States of America

British Library Cataloguing in Publication Data
Data available

Library of Congress Cataloging in Publication Data
Data available

Original Series, 60

ISBN 978-0-85-991833-6

INTRODUCTION.

I. DESCRIPTION OF THE MS.

THE MS. from which the poem here presented to the reader has been copied is known as Harl. MS. 1701, and marked Plut. LXXII. B. The volume, which is about 12 in. × 9 in., contains three poems:

    a. *Handlyng Synne*,
    b. *The Medytacyuns*,
    c. *Roberd of Cyssille*.

The first two leaves are blank; *a.* occupies 83 leaves and part of the 84th, ending in the second column of the first side of leaf 84. It is immediately followed by our poem, which, it will be seen, commences in the second column of leaf 84. It closes on the second page of leaf 91 (fol. 91, back), of which it occupies somewhat more than half. On leaf 92 commences *Kyng Roberd of Cyssille*, which closes on the first side of leaf 95.

The headings of the divisions of the poem are all written in red ink; a few of the capitals are illuminated, and the lines are all bracketed in pairs with red ink. In "the fourþe poynt of þe soper" five ¶'s have been introduced, but whether by the original scribe or by a later one I am unable to say: they are done in blue. The handwriting is very regular and very clear; a few omissions occur, but nearly all have been supplied by the original scribe with the usual mark (ʌ) underneath. These are all noted, as well as a few which I have thought to be required: one whole line has been supplied from the Bodleian MS.

vi INTRODUCTION. I. DESCRIPTION OF THE MS.

A few words have their meanings written over them, thus :—

	wrappe		euer
l. 345	mode	l. 1030	ay
	place		soper
l. 440	ce to ce	l. 1111	cene
	haste		take
l. 821	reke	l. 1114	nome

The punctuation of the MS. is so very slight, that it has been disregarded altogether. I have expanded the contractions where I could see clearly what was intended, and håve marked the expansions according to our custom. In a few cases the mark of contraction seemed doubtful, and these I have noted at the foot of the page where they occur. Frequently *gh* has a mark through it, thus, gh̄, and it will be found so printed in the text, even where it perhaps ought to be followed by a *t*: thus tagh̄ in the MS. is not expanded into tagh̄*t*; and thogh̄ is printed thogh̄ without any expansion. In line 554 the words "crucyfye, crucyfye" have a slight curl, or it may be *g*, over the *ye*; a curl somewhat similar is found over such a word as "our," which I have expanded into our*e*; but the word "crucyfye" I have left. MS. B. has "crucyfige." The word is in the imperative mood, singular; and "crucyfye" or "crucyfyge" will correspond with the grammar of the poem, as will be seen further on.

The only other known copy of the poem is in the Bodl. MS. 415, which also contains the *Handlyng Synne*. Mr Geo. Parker of Oxford has kindly read my transcript with the Bodleian MS., and noted all the variations between the two. They are but slight, but the Bodl. MS. has supplied one whole line (248) as stated before, and correct readings in ll. 214, 216; while l. 1102 seems to be corrupt in both MSS.

II. GRAMMATICAL NOTES.

The few notes I have made upon the grammatical forms of this poem are such as presented themselves to my mind in reading the MS., aided by a hint from the Rev. W. W. Skeat, which is referred to below. The forms I have tabulated are intended for those readers who are interested in the grammar of our language, and they will, I trust, be of some use to those who are more competent than I am to

INTRODUCTION. II. GRAMMATICAL NOTES. vii

draw correct conclusions as to the date of the poem and the locality in which it was written. My object has been simply to tabulate forms; and if at any time I have ventured to give utterance to an opinion of my own, or to deduce any principle from the facts before me, I have done so with the utmost deference to the opinions of others.

1. VERBS.

(i.) Verbs in the third person singular, indicative mood, present tense, end generally in *eth*, some few in *th*; as :—

wytnesseþ	l. 51		kalleþ	l. 535
putteþ	71		goþ	571
boweþ	148		bereþ	572
wasseþ	151		suffyseþ	693
cleppeþ	152		endyþ	775
kysseþ	152		suffreþ	782
governeþ	211		wexyþ	825
foloweþ	295		seeþ	848
preyeþ	310		accepteþ	913
kepeþ	404		answereþ	1004
seyþ	408		shameþ	1081
cumþ	418		ȝyfþ	1106
chargeþ	470		cryeþ	1106
wadeþ	520		geþ	1122
sheweþ	524			

Once only have I noticed the verb in the *second* person singular, indicative, present tense, to end in *th* :—

" Fy ! þat goddes temple *dystroyþ* " (674).

(ii.) Verbs in the third person plural, present indicative, end in *eth* and in *en*. The following end in *eth* :—

bygynneþ [1]	p. 1		scorneþ	l. 429
blyndyþ	l. 427		syngeþ	429
boffeteþ	428		dyspyseþ	673
seyþ	428		seeþ	848

The following end in *n*, *en* :—

ben	l. 122		pycchen	l. 612
sen	232		cleuyn	616
crepyn	286		beren	667
callen	292		doun	755
deluyn	347, 611		dyen	755
axen	430		lakkyn	884
leyn	521		wounden	911
dryuen	593		wrastyn	911
dyggen	611		shullen	1108

---

[1] In B. *bygynnen*

(iii.) Imperatives in the singular have two terminations -*e* (sometimes omitted), and *th* in the proportion of rather more than two of the former to one of the latter. Bearing in mind Mr Skeat's distinction between "thou and ye" in *William of Palerne* (Intro. xli), I have endeavoured to classify these imperatives to see whether the author followed any definite system in their use.[1] At first all seems confusion—*e* and þ being apparently used indiscriminately.

Omitting the expletives "þenk"(e), "beþenk"(e), and "beholde," used only by the translator to his reader, which never end in þ, they may be divided thus :—

(*a*) The translator addressing the reader, *or equal addressing equal*, uses the *e* termination generally, as :—

say	l. 8	receyue	l. 218
opone	10	here	219
hyde	10	do	298
take	17, 43, 297, 371	loþe	299
loke	167	crucyfye	608
haue	179	so	826

Christ addressing His Father—*Equals*—also uses the *e* termination :—

kepe	l. 259, 354, 366, 368	ryse	l. 338
bowe	312	forgyue	649, 711
lestene	312	graunte	650
here	313	saue	651
dyspyse	313	slake	696
see	316	take	746

The Father to the Son—*Equals* :—

Com	l. 750	sytte	l. 754
Come	754		

The Virgin to death :—

Come	l. 791	do	l. 792

The Virgin to her Son :—

haue reuþe on me l. 832

The mob to Christ :—

telle who þe smyt	l. 428	saue þy selfe	l. 675
Come to þy dome	483	come adowne	676

The Virgin to the disciples :—

dysmay ʒow nat l. 1090

St Michael to Christ in His agony :—

oumforte þe weyl l. 398   do manly l. 398

---

[1] I am reminded that *ye* for *thou* is regularly Northern; it is first found in the *Tristrem*, then in the *Haveluk*.

INTRODUCTION. II. GRAMMATICAL NOTES. ix

The last two ought, perhaps, to be classed with the following three,
as exceptions to the rule :—

  Be   l. 2   graunte l. 5
  saue   4

These occur in the translator's invocation to the Deity. And lastly,
se, 701, used by the Virgin to God. This may be an error of the
scribe, as Mary, we shall see, in every other instance uses the
termination *th*.

We may then, I think, conclude that equals address equals
without the final *th*.

(*b*) I come now to examine the imperatives which end in *th*.
Among these are no expletives to be struck out.

Christ addressing His disciples, Superior addressing inferiors,
use *th* :—

  makeþ l. 196 weteþ l. 254
  kepeþ   247 aryseþ   280

The Virgin, apparently assuming superiority, says to the women,
seeþ (809); to the disciples :—

  takeþ l. 950 lateþ l. 994
  beryeþ   951 douteþ 1105
  abydeþ 991, 1047 beþ   1107
  goþ   994

The Virgin to the Jews who came to remove the bodies from the
cross :—

  pyneþ l. 847 ȝrueþ l. 848
  brekeþ   847 haueþ   850

In these last instances, although the Virgin appears as a sup-
pliant, yet we cannot doubt but that the poet intended to represent
her as the superior of the "houndes" who came to break the legs of
those hanging on the cross, and to cast their bodies into the ditch
close by. Once, as we have seen (1090), Mary uses "dysmay"
when addressing the disciples, and only once. John, too, uses the
forms under notice twice; once, addressing these same Jews at the
cross, he says, "goþ hens" (873), and again, in addressing the
women, "beþe of gode cumforte" (895). A seeming inconsistency
appears in this last, but it must be remembered that to him was
given the care of the Virgin; and with this charge he seems to have
had the care and command of all the women.

INTRODUCTION. II. GRAMMATICAL NOTES.

So far, then, we should be tolerably safe in saying equals addressed equals without the *th*, and superiors inferiors with it; but another class will compel us to modify what would have been a convenient division, and one which could have been accounted for by *number* (as the division, perhaps, will be after all), namely, that imperatives singular end in *e*, while in the plural they end in *th*. The class which remains for examination is that in which inferiors address superiors.

The Virgin in her prayer to God uses

kepeþ	l. 458	ȝeldeþ	l. 468
beþ	459	helpeþ	471
doþ	465	bryngeþ	472
lateþ	467		

Broadly stated, then, we may say, equals address equals in *e*, and unequals address unequals in *th*.

We may also say that all imperatives in *e* (except dysmay followed by the pronoun) are in the singular number, and that all in *th*—nine exceptions—are in the plural number.[1]

(iv.) A few verbs occur in the second person indicative, terminating in *est*, as : þenkest (21), takest (202), seest (205), forsakest (727), betakest (728), suffrest (868), and sentest (317). We have also byt for bade (305), and byst for biddest (1015); fynst for findest (557), shust for shouldest (714), and bynte for bind (427).

(v.) The present participle ends in *ing* (yng) throughout; to this I find no exceptions; unless memorand, ll. 32 and 195, are taken as participles.

II. NOUNS.

Of Nouns not much need be said. Generally the plural ends in *s*, *es*, or *ys*, as opynyon*s*, wurd*es*, herty*s*; but a few end in *en*, as :—

teren, tears	l. 634	sostryn, sisters	l. 647
yen, eyes	357	shamen, shames	672
breþren	647	houden, hands	912

The possessive (several exceptions) ends in *s*, *es*, *ys*, as :—

Martyals legende	l. 51	goddes grace	l. 9
Sones passyun	3	crystys passyun	14

---

[1] See *Morris's Specimens of Early English*, Introduction, xxxiii.

III. Pronouns.

The Personal Pronouns are, Singular--

1.	2.	3.
y	þou	he, she (also se), hyt
my, myn	þy, þyn	hys, here
me	þe	hym, here, hyt

Plural—

1.	2.	3.
we	ȝe	þey
oure	ȝoure	here
vs	ȝow	hem

The interrogatives *who* (106, 551) and *ho* (526, 790) occur; also the relatives *whiche* (812) and *þat* (215). *He* occurs once as a neuter unless we say 'world' is masculine:—

<blockquote>
And ȝyf þe worlde ȝow hate now,
Weteþ þat <i>he</i> me hated ar ȝow (253-4).
</blockquote>

Here I cannot do better than quote Mr Skeat's remarks on the use of *Thou* and *Ye* before referred to. He says, "*Thou* is the language of a lord to a servant, of an equal to an equal, and expresses also companionship, love, permission, defiance, scorn, threatening; whilst *ye* is the language of a servant to a lord, and of compliment, and further expresses honour, submission, entreaty."[1] A careful examination of the pronouns used in this poem gives the same results. Thus, Christ addresses His Father as *Thou*, *Thee*—using ȝow once in the accusative (314)—or in the language of an "equal to an equal." The author addresses his reader in the same terms—*thou, thee*.

The Jews, in "scorn," address Jesus as *Thou* (436-8). John, as the beloved companion of Christ, uses *thee*—"who shal þe betrey?" (106). St Michael, who was sent from heaven to comfort the Saviour, uses at first the language of a "servant"—"for ȝow we (the angels) preyd" (382); but afterwards he uses that of love—*thee* (383). He again uses *thee*, but he seems to be repeating the Father's words (403).

Mary, using "the language of a servant to a lord," and expressing at the same time "honour, submission, and entreaty," in her prayer to the Father in heaven, uses *ye, you, youre*, with the plural verbs (457—469).

[1] *William of Palerne*, Intro. xlii.

The translator twice uses *you* when addressing Christ (579-80), and John uses *ye* to Mary (853).

IV. ADJECTIVES.

The comparative in *er* occurs in logher (133), and the superlative in *est* in ʒungest (56).

V. ADVERBS.

In adverbs we have *nygh* (90) and *ny* (418, 566) with the comparative *ner* (584). Once the adverb terminates in *lygh*, gladlygh (89); in all other instances in *ly*, as shamely (172), manly (398).

To conclude. The results of this examination show that

1. Verbs in the third person singular, present, indicative mood, end in *eth*. This termination is Southern and East Midland.[1]

2. Verbs in the third person plural, indicative mood, end in *eth* or in *en*; the number having the latter ending being eighteen, that of the former only eight: *eth* is the Southern ending; *en* is the Midland ending.[2]

3. Verbs in the second person singular, indicative mood, end in *est*. This termination is Southern and East Midland.[3]

4. Verbs imperative, singular, end in *e*, except some few particularly mentioned above; the imperative plural, second person, with one exception, in *eth*; (but note "þank we" and "gyn we" in ll. 1133, 1135, which are 1st pers. pl.)

5. The present participles end in *ing*, which is Southern,[4] but had spread over the Midland by 1310, as we see in the rimes in the *Handlyng Synne*.

6. Nouns plural end in *es*, *ys*, some few in *en*.

From all which we conclude the language is Midland, with some Southern forms, due, most likely, to the transcriber.

III. AUTHORSHIP, ETC.

The numerous translations of S. Bonaventura's *Vita Christi* which exist show how popular the work has always been. The partial translation here for the first time printed is probably the earliest in existence. The next in order would seem to be one

---

[1] *Specimens of E. E. Poetry*, xii.   [2] Ibid.
[3] Ibid. In the *Havelok* we find "Thou sittes."   [4] *Genesis and Exodus*, xxviii.

mentioned in Lowndes' *Bib. Manual* under the title of *The Myrrour of the blessyed Life of Ihesu Cryst*, translated into English in the year 1410, and printed by Richard Pynson.[1] In the British Museum are two copies, printed by Caxton in 1488, one on paper, the other on vellum. There is also in the Museum a copy printed by W. de Worde in 1525. The only copies of modern editions which I have seen are one published in London in 1739, translated and edited by "E. Y." and another published at Frome Selwood for the use of Members of the Church of England, so recently as 1868. This appears without translator's or editor's name.[2] "E. Y." speaks of an "Obsolete Edition" which he intended to copy, merely altering the orthography; but finding the "Editor (of this Obsolete Edition) having often through the whole omitted many Passages of the Saint, and inserted others in their Room, such as were either agreeable with his own Thoughts, or collected from other Authors, who have wrote on the same Subject," he determined on a new translation. To what "obsolete edition" he refers I cannot say, nor can I ascertain who "E. Y." was.

Robert Mannyng of Bourne, in Lincolnshire, was probably the translator of the *Medytacyuns*. In 1303 he translated *Le Manuel des Pechiez* under the title of *Handlyng Synne*. In the Harl. MS. our poem immediately follows the *Handlyng Synne*, and in the Bodleian the two also appear together. Between 1327 and 1338 Mannyng translated Peter de Langtoft's French *Chronicle* into English, and possibly he may, about this time, have made a translation of a portion of Bonaventura's *Meditationes Vitæ Christi*.[3]

As bearing upon the authorship, we may say it is well known that Mannyng used to take great liberties with his originals. A glance at Mr Furnivall's *Handlyng Synne* will show to how great an extent he introduced original stories to illustrate some point which he deemed of importance. The same thing will be found here. Among passages which do not appear in the Latin original may be noted the following :—

[1] Bohn's *Lowndes' Bib. Man.*, p. 234.
[2] The Catalogue says it is by the Rev. F. Oakeley.
[3] Mr T. L. Kington Oliphant thinks Manning wrote the *Handlyng Synne* from 1303—1310; and that he then began the present poem.

xiv INTRODUCTION. III. AUTHORSHIP.

The opening part, consisting of 22 lines, is wholly the translator's own. Lines 130, 136, 138, and 170,

þat þe lered men shulde teche the lewed,

are also interpolations.

Lines 212, 215, 217, and 218 are new, and noteworthy, as showing the opinion of the translator upon an important doctrine :—

He þat þou seest yn þe prestes fest.	212
He þat þou seest yn forme of brede,	215
Hyt ys goddys sone quyk nat ded.	
With clene herte þou hym receyue,	217
For elles þy soule þou wylt deceyue.	218

The expression "tyl þat he wax hote" (369), and that Christ suffered in His agony only in His Manhood and not in His Godhead (411-12), are also new; as are lines 477-8,

Both bollers of wyne and eche a gadlyng
Come oute for to se of Ihesus endyng;

and the exclamation (529-30),

Almyȝty god! where art þou now?
þese houndes seme myȝtyer þan þou!

In the "third hour" the expressive lines (567-8) are due to the translator :—

þey punged hym furþe þurgh euery slogh,
As an hors ys prykked þat goþ yn þe plogh.

As he went on the translator took greater liberties, and introduced more of his own matter, and generally with advantage. Thus, after l. 768 had said the Saviour's dying cry was heard in hell, we have added :—

þenk now, man, what ioye þere ys
Whan soules ben broȝt from pyne to blys.
A! how long þey haue þere lyue,
To abyde here sauyour yn many a pyne;
þey cleped, and cryed, com goddes sone,
How long shul we yn þys wo wone?

And further on, after l. 834, the following new matter is introduced :—

To þe cros foote hastly she ran,
And clypped þe cros faste yn here arme,
And seyd, my sone here wyl y dey,
Ar þou from me be bore aweye.

After the Saviour's death and the appearance of the water and blood, the translator breaks out (861-8) :—

AA, wrong! aa, wo! aa, wykkednes!
To martyre here for here mekenes.
Þe sone was dede, he felte no smerte,
But certes hyt perced þe modyrs hert.
Þey wounded here, and heped harm vp on harmes;
She fyl, as for dede, yn maudeleyns armys.
A! Ihesu, þys dede ys ful wundyr to me,
Þat þou suffrest þy modyr be martyred for þe.

The line commencing "She fyl" only being in the original. Omitting the inserted lines 879-882 and 923-4, we arrive at a longer passage, which also seems worthy of being introduced here:—

Feyn wulde she ha bore more of here dere sone,
But grete sorowe here strengþe had ouercome.
Þat arme wepyng ofte she kyste,
She kolled hyt, she clypped hyt vp on here brest.
But euer whan she behelde þat grysly wounde,
For sorowe & for feyntnes she fyl to þe grounde.
Oftyn she seyd a, sone! a, sone!
Where ys now alle þat werk become,
Þat þou were wunt to werche with þys honde?
Feuers and syke men to brynge oute of bonde.
A, flesshe! a, fode! moste feyre and most fre,
Of þe holy goste conceyued yn me,
Why fadest þou? no fylþe yn þe ys founde,
For synneles y bare þe yn to þys mounde.
A! mannes synne dere hast þou boȝt,
With a gretter prys myȝt hyt neuer be boȝt.—ll. 929-944.

The whole of the final Meditation, except the idea in ll. 1126-29, is due to the translator. Of other liberties, such as the expansion or condensation of the original, it would be too tedious to speak—the handling throughout has been free,—the translator following his own judgment wherever he deemed it best.[1]

R. Mannyng's desire to teach the lewed will be well remembered. He translated Langtoft's *Chronicle* into "*symple speche*" "*for the luf of symple men*," and in "light lange" he it "*beganne, for luf of the lewed manne;*" and here, in the *Medytacyuns*, we have

A feyre monasshyng hys sermoun shewed
Þat þe lered men shulde teche þe lewed.[2]

One other parallel passage may be quoted. In *Handlyng Synne* we meet with this:—

Whan Iesu deyde thurghe passyun
Hys dyscyplys doutede echoun

---

[1] Miss L. Toulmin Smith read my proof with the Latin Original.
[2] ll. 169, 170.

> Whether he shulde ryse or noun.
> Alle that beleuede yn hym byfore,
> Alle here beleue was nyghe forlore
> Fro the fryday that he deyde
> To tyme that he ros, as he seyde.
> But hys modyr vyrgyne Marie,
> Hho bare the beleue vp stedfastly
> Fro the fryday at the noun
> Tyl alle the satyrday was doun,
> And alle the nyght tyle that he ros.[1]

With this compare ll. 1107, 1110 of the *Medytacyuns*. Addressing the weeping disciples, Mary says :—

> Beeþ of gode cumfort, for trustly y say,
> We shullen hym se on þe þrydde day;
> Seþþen he haþ boght vs at so grete prys,
> Nedes from þe deþ he mote aryse.

Against these in favour of Mannyng being the translator we must place the undoubted difference of dialect between the *Medytacyuns* and the *Chronicle*. By the kindness of Mr Furnivall I have been supplied with some forward sheets of his forthcoming edition of Brunne's translation of Langtoft's *Chronicle*, and have made a careful examination of 2230 lines (all I had), or of a portion about twice the length of the *Medytacyuns*. I have shown in the grammatical notes to this poem[2] that the dialect is E. Midland. Availing myself of Mr Morris's tests I have obtained the following results respecting the dialect of the *Chronicle*:—

1. Verbs in the third person singular, indicative, end (with a very few exceptions) in *es*. This is the Northern or W. Midland form.[3]

2. Verbs in the third person plural, indicative, end in *s* or *es* (except one or two). This also is the Northern or W. Midland termination.[3]

3. Verbs of the second person singular, present, indicative, end in *es* and *est*, two of the latter to three of the former; again showing in favour of a Northern dialect.

4. Imperatives singular are but few, and show no partiality for any particular dialect; but the imperatives plural mostly end in *es*; that is, have a Northern or W. Midland ending.

5. Present or imperfect participles end in *and*, *ande*, and *yng*.

---

[1] *Handlyng Synne*, Furnivall's ed., p. 29.   [2] Ante, p. xii.
[3] These forms are also found in the E. Midland *Havelok*.

6. Nouns plural generally end in *es;* none I think in *en.*

There are other details which point strongly to a Northern rather than a Southern influence; such as the use of *hepen* and *þeþen,* which are said to be "unknown to the Southern dialect;"[1] the constant occurrence of *til* (to) as a preposition; and other forms which I need not specify. So marked a difference in dialect can only be accounted for, supposing the *Chronicle* and the *Medytacyuns* proceeded from the same man, by the liberties taken by transcribers with their originals. It was only natural that, when they copied a work, they should endeavour to adapt the language to the district in which it was to be used.

It is matter for regret that these *Meditations* have not been in the hands of subscribers and students earlier. I copied the MS., and this Introduction was written, some five years ago—want of funds on the one hand, and my absence from England on the other, have delayed its appearance until now. During my brief holiday I have done what little I could (imperfectly, I know) to finish Henry Brinklow's volume for the student of history, and these *Meditations* for those especially who care to go back to "The sources of Standard English."[2]

J. M. COWPER.

Watling Street, Canterbury,
February 23, 1875.

Mr T. L. Kington Oliphant has read the proof of the *Medytacyuns,* and has kindly made the following notes:—

"I think there is no doubt that the 'Soper' must have been compiled by Robert of Brunne. The following are expressions that also come in the *Handlyng Synne:*—

"Page (Soper) 30. God *ones* (olim) said; also, *swyche, same, nat only, smert, afore, pens, tugge, holy* (omnino), *the which, ho* (quis), *wuld God, seced* (cessavit). There is the same fondness for *gh* instead of the old *h,* as *logher, syghyng, þogh, Myghel, þurgh, glad-*

---
[1] Morris's *Specimens, &c.,* xv.
[2] The title of Mr Oliphant's most useful book.

lygh. There is, in common with the Northern Psalter, *bie* (emere), *wicked* (with the *d* at the end), *thos* = *thes* (illi), p. 19, *them which* (p. 9).

"*Astyte* is a regular Northern expression; *teit* comes in the Haveloc; so does *stone dead.*

"*Furthermore* is in the Tristrem. There are many expressions found in the Cursor Mundi (Northern Version, which I think Dr Morris dates about 1290). These are *tite*, p. 268; *rife*, p. 18; *put* (in the sense of *ponere*), p. 96; (Ormin's) *bad* (jussit), p. 108; *cole* (occidere), p. 166; *ha* instead of *have*, p. 22; *wunt*, p. 208; *you* for *thou*, p. 164; *cors* (corpus) is also used in both works. Stratmann gives none but Northern examples of this last.

"There are some new expressions in the Soper, such as *bring about, swoon* (the *n* at the end is here first found); *stuck*, from *stikien* (p. 29); *grub*, for pluck up; *hereupon, strait* to hell (p. 35); *by cause* (quia); *most* is used for the superlative, p. 15. We see *a by path*, 16, like Manning's *bi way; to lay on* (thrash), *own self* (line 680). The Northern *them*, not *hem*, comes in p. 12, and has not been altered by the transcriber. The East Anglian *clad* is found in p. 16. The 3 pers. sing. in *es* comes often, like *hangis* (pendet).

"The word *preyour* (p. 13) altered to suit the rime is odd. The Southern transcriber was most likely a Kentishman, for we find *a ver* (afar), p. 19. He has *teren* (lachryme), *some seyþ*, was *ibroke*, and many such.

"The different reading *nor* in p. 2 is a sure mark of the North; it is never found in the South East about 1360, which I suppose is the date of the transcription."

ADDITIONS FOR *MEDITATIONS*.

NO. 60, ORIGINAL SERIES.

VARIOUS READINGS OF A MS. IN TRIN. COLL. CAMB. B. 14. 19.

BY THE REV. J. R. LUMBY, B.D.[1]

Line	16.	... þei may lere.
,,	18.	But þat þat is proved of cristis fay.
,,	38.	þat in þis cene crist haþ wrouȝt,
,,	40.	þe secounde his disciplis waischyng.
,,	46.	To make redi his pask aȝenus he come.
,,	49.	... as þou herd seie.
,,	54.	... þei saten him bi.
,,	58.	So trist so trewe as was Joon.
,,	73.	... men han seen.
,,	74.	... of Laterain
,,	75.	An oþer manere þou understonde.
,,	80.	To slepen on his brest Ioon þau liste.
,,	86.	For as a seruaunt ...
,,	92.	Crist seide þese wordis wiþ sad chere.
,,	95.	Forsoþe forsoþe I wole ȝou seie.
,,	101.	For ye *this MS always spells* iȝe.
,,	105.	Priueli Ioon to crist gan seie.
,,	127.	Biholde and þenke þis in þi mynde.
,,	133.	To an inner hous gunnen þanne tee.
		So seyn þat þe houshold hanne see.
		He dide hem sitten adoun in þat stide.
,,	166.	Whanne he waischide ...
,,	175.	In stidfast praier ...
,,	178.	Into his blis þei wolen þee lede.
,,	180.	Hou dereworþili aforn his ende
,,	181.	*om.* with.
,,	183.	*alþer* in one word. It is genitive plural of *all*, and probably is only written *divisim* here by accident.
,,	185.	... he gan sowne.
,,	195.	In memoraunce ...
,,	203.	... more cleer.

[1] Mr Lumby also notes that there is a prose version of the *Meditations* in the Bodleian MS. 789 (new number: 2643 in the ordinary catalogue), leaves 1-51, bk; and that the tract "To kunne deie" in the same volume is of worth for its dialect.

ADDITIONS FOR *MEDITATIONS*, NO. 60, ORIGINAL SERIES.

Line	207.	From hevene he list ...
,,	214.	To ʒyve þee peyne ...
,,	216.	... quyk not deed.
,,	245.	þe þridde he tauʒte hem bi monesting To kepyng his comaunding
,,	264.	þat schulen ...
,,	267.	þese wordis and oþere þat he hem tolde kitten her hertis and waxen coolde.
,,	271.	... wiþ manye siʒyng.
,,	277.	þis sermoun at his brest he souke.
,,	283.	Forþ þei wente ...
,,	286.	As chikenes crepten to þe dammes wyng
,,	291.	Faste þei wenten þei camen anoon.
,,	295.	*om.* yn.
,,	299.	Schame ...
,,	300.	For he schamed not to die for þee
,,	305.	He biddiþ ...
,,	328.	... have ʒolden a stounde.
,,	336.	þei han me prisid my woo to make.
,,	347.	... delven ...
,,	356.	He foond hem slepyng and summe he woke Her iʒen weren slepyng ...
,,	362.	... and dide more
,,	372.	... praie þi god above.
,,	406.	To my fadir in his sete.
,,	414.	Al bisprongen ...
,,	427.	Summe bynden summe blenden him sum on him spit Summe buffetiden him and summe seyn telle who þe smyt Summe scornen him sum syngen on hym a song.
,,	436.	þerfor þou schalt have deþ as riʒt
,,	438.	Help þi silf if þou be boun.
,,	441.	Summe drugge him summe drawe him fro see to see.
,,	450.	þei wepen þei weilen her wristis þei wryngen.
,,	464.	Be brouʒt
,,	473.	Thenke man and rewe of her sekyng
,,	477.	Boþe lorels and ech gadlynge.
,,	490.	Aswoun sche fel doun in þe feeld. þanne crist was torment in moost care.
,,	502.	þo was maad frenschip þere firste was bate.
,,	505.	þei crieden on him as foule on owle.
,,	516.	þei beten him and renten hym wounde to wounde.
,,	520.	Biholdiþ he ...
,,	522.	Til þei ben weeri þei moun no more.
,,	538.	þe doyng of þe þridde our now wole I ryme.
,,	541.	... a reehed þei took.
,,	543.	þei setten hym openli in her clepyng

ADDITIONS FOR *MEDITATIONS*, NO. 60, ORIGINAL SERIES.

Line	546.	þou modi man þi sauyour biholde
,,	548.	And for oo word þou woldist men grame
		Eft soone to pilat þei camen accusyng
		And seiden saif sir Cesar we han no kyng.
,,	567.	þei punchid him forþ þorou ilke a slowȝ
,,	573.	þei hiȝen hym he goiþ wiþouten striif
,,	583.	... foloweþ a fer.
,,	585.	A schort weie sche is goon to chese.
,,	599.	For evere it semeþ aȝenus his wille.
,,	627.	To þe cross forth þei drowen him defiyng.
,,	632.	A schortere laddere biforn was set,
		þere as þe feet schortere weren.
,,	637.	Wiþout aȝen seiyng ...
,,	642.	... crucifieris hem bereiȝt.
,,	648.	... be merciful ...
,,	654.	þat oon Jew ...
,,	655.	þe oþere him drowen til veynes to brest.
,,	663.	Eueri ioynt þanne brast atwynne.
,,	702.	I praie þee somdeel hise peynes lisse.
,,	715.	... was nome.
,,	728.	... me takist.
,,	733.	He taastiþ sumdeel his preste to liþen.
,,	737.	ȝit treuli man þirstide on rode.
,,	746.	... calle me to þee.
,,	760.	... I take.
,,	763.	... centurio gan torne.
,,	812.	Whiche I bar wemles of mij bodi.
,,	817.	... grete sone ...
,,	823.	To sle hem and caste her cors awei
		þat noon schulde se hem on sabat dai
,,	835.	... scharpli sche ran.
,,	856.	... þorow merci ...
,,	859.	þorou out his herte he prcent him wiþ mood.
,,	888.	If we goon hennes þis bodi worþ stole
,,	896.	Joseph of Armathie ...
,,	934.	... for feyntise ...
,,	944.	A grettir pris myȝte nevere be brouȝte.
,,	949.	... seide marie ...
,,	960.	Prikid, brisid ...
,,	990.	And greiþide hem faste þennis to goon.
,,	1007.	But I hadde trist to his seying
		Myn herte schulde aborst at his diing.
,,	1015.	I must do nedis as þou me biddest.
,,	1023.	... now departid.
,,	1027.	If þou risist up as þou me behiȝtist
		Myn herte schal rise wiþ þe liȝtest
,,	1030.	I am stoon deed for oones and ay

ADDITIONS FOR *MEDITATIONS*, NO. 60, ORIGINAL SERIES.

Line 1032. And kiþe þat þou art goddis sone.
„ 1034. Sche romyde ...
„ 1047. Sche sai þe cros : Abide, sche seide
„ 1087. ... maistras.
„ 1118. ... he soukide it ...
„ 1123. Fro fendis bounde to make þee free.

ADDITIONAL NOTES BY THE REV. W. W. SKEAT, M.A.

Line 328. Read 'a stounde,' two words. At any rate, it means 'at any time.'
„ 414. Read 'be-sprunge,' with a hyphen.
„ 513. Read 'vndyr-neme,' with a hyphen.
„ 570. Read 'a-sterte,' with a hyphen.
„ 577. Dele comma after 'owne.'
Lines 632, 633. The full stop should be at the end of l. 633, and the comma at the end of l. 632.
Line 918. Observe that here only *one* nail is used for fastening the feet. So in Piers the Plowman—'nailede hym with *thre* nayles,' C. xxi. 51.

In the Glossary, note the following corrections :—

Angred means afflicted, not made sorry, and refers to the infliction of pain. The use of *anger* in the sense of affliction, pain, is curious, yet common. See *anger* in Stratmann.
Astounde, at any time (for *a stounde*), 328.
Besprunge, besprinkled, 414. Wrongly entered as *Sprunge*.
Cleuyn, cleave, 616. *Cleuyn on* = cleave to, cling to.
Fode, a child, 939. *Omitted*.
Iuwyse, instrument of punishment, 577. It commonly means punishment only, as in Chaucer's Knightes Tale.
Knowlechyng, recognition, 424. To *knowleche* is to recognize, to acknowledge ; not 'to *know*.'
Kyþe, make manifest, shew, 1032. Not 'to *know*.'
Myþe, meek, mild, 156. See *Methe* in Halliwell. (Certainly not *mighty*.)
Owne, own ; not 'only.'
Real, royal, 640. So also in ll. 33, 34. (The usual meaning.)
Ryue, rife (in great numbers, or else quickly), 839.
Seche, to seek, 621. It simply means to seek, examine.
Soke, sucked, 1118. *Omitted*.
Too, 654. The too = thet oo, the one. (Very common.)
Vndyrneme, reprove, 513. See *Vnderneme* in Prompt. Parv.; and cf. P. Pl. B. v. 115.

[*Harl. MS.* 1701, *leaf* 84, *col.* 1.]

Here bygynnep¹ medytacyuns of þe soper of [leaf 84]
oure lorde Ihesu. And also of hys pas-
syun. And eke of þe peynes of hys
swete modyr, Mayden marye. Þe
whyche made yn latyn Bonauenture Car-
dynall.

Alle my3ty god yn trynyte,
   Now & euer wyþ vs be;   God be with us,
   For þy sones passyun
Saue alle þys congregacyun;   4
And graunte vs grace of gode lyuyng   and grant us bliss.
To wynne vs blysse wyþouten endyng.
Now euery man, yn hys degre,
Sey amen, amen, pur charyte.   8
Thou crysten creature, by goddes grace,   Christian,
Opone þyn herte and hyde þy face;   open thy heart.
For þou shalt chaunge þy chere a none,
Or elles þyn herte ys harder þan stone.   12
Y wyl þe lere a medytacyun   I will teach thee
Compyled of crystys passyun;   a meditation of the Passion.
And of hys modyr, þat ys² dere,
What peynes þey suffred þou mayst lere.   16
Take hede, for y wyl no þyng seye
But þat ys preued by crystes feye,   May be proved by Holy Writ or
By holy wryt, or seyntes sermons,   Saints' sermons.
Or by dyuers holy opynyons.   20

   ¹ bygynnen   ² ys so

No fiend will annoy thee. [leaf 81, col. 2]	Whan þou þenkest þys yn þy þoȝt Thyr may no fende noye þe with noȝt.¹

Now of þe soper of oure lorde Ihesu.

God sent His Son to save mankind.	Comyng þe tyme of grete mercy, Whan god sent hys sone down² fro³ hy, Of a mayden he wulde be bore, To saue mankynde þat was forlore.	24
He would not "buy" us with silver and gold, but with His blood.	But noþer with corupt syluer ne⁴ golde; But wyþ hys blode, by⁵ vs he wulde.	28
He made a Supper for a memorial.	Whan tyme was come to suffre þys A soper he made to hys dycyplys; Are he were ded and shuld fro⁶ hem wende, A memorand þyng to haue yn mynde.	32
This Supper was real.	Þys soper was real as þou mayst here, Foure real þynges cryst made þere.	
Think upon it, and God will not let thee go fasting.	Ȝyf þou þenke weyl on þys fedyng, God wyl nat late þe passe fastyng.	36
Four things to be had in mind.	Foure þynges þou most haue yn þy þoȝt, Þat yn þys soper cryst haþ wroȝt:	
First, a bodily feeding. Second, the feet washing. Third, Himself in Bread, Fourth, a Sermon.	Þe fyrst ys a bodly⁷ fedyng, Þe secunde ys ⁸hys dycyples fete⁸ wasshyng, Þe þred yn brede hym self takyng, Þe fourþe a sermoun of feyre makyng.	40

The fyrst poynt of þe soper.

The first "point."	Now to þe fyrst:—take gode entent	
He sent Peter and John to prepare the Supper. [leaf 81, back]	How petyr and iohne from hym he sent, Yn to þe mounte of syon, To greyþe hys paske aȝens ne com.	44
On Thursday night He came with His disciples.	And on a þursday pedyr he lyȝt Wyþ hys dycyplys aȝens nyȝt.	48
The Supper was prepared by the 72 disciples.	Þe soper was dyȝt, as y herd sey,	

¹ oght   ² down *comes after* sent *in* B.   ³ from   ⁴ nor
⁵ bie   ⁶ from   ⁷ bodyly   ⁸ *om.*

By dyscyplys seuenty and twey;
Seynt Martyals legende wytnesseþ ryȝt,
With hem he was þe soper to dyȝt.   52   S. Martial's legend.
Whan þe soper was made redy,   When supper was ready,
Cryst sette hym down, and þey hym by;   Christ sat down;
Iohne þe euangelyst sate hym nexte,   John sat next to Him.
Al þogħ he were of age ȝungeste;   56
To hym was none of hem echone   None so true as John.
So trusty and so trewe as was Iohne:
For fere wulde he nat fle hym fro,   He would not flee till Christ
Tyl he was ded and byryed also.   60   was buried.
Byholde now, man, and þou shalt se
How euery man sate yn hys degre.
Here table was brode and foure square,   The table was four-square.
The maner of þat¹ cuntre was swych þare;   64
On euery syde sate of hem þre,   Three sat on each side and Christ
And cryst yn a corner mekely to se: in a corner.
So þat here by þou mayst lere   Hereby thou mayest learn how
þat of o dysshe þey etyn yn fere,   68   they could eat out of one dish.
þarfore þe myȝt nat vndyrstonde
Whan cryst seyd, "he þat hys honde
Yn my dysshe putteþ furþ ryȝt,
He shal betraye me þys nyȝt."   72
Thys table at rome men haue seyn,   This table men have seen at
Yn seynt Iohne chyrche þe latereyn.   Rome. [See *Stacions of Rome*, ed. Furnivall.]
A nouþer maner mayst þou vndyrstande,
þat þey stonde with staues yn honde,   76   They eat standing to fulfil Moses' Law,
Etyng faste, and stondyng stylle,
Moyses lawe to fulfylle.
Cryst lete hem sytte, so semeþ best,   but Christ lets them sit.
For elles ne had Ione slept one hys brest.   80
When graces were seyd, and alle men sette,   "Graces" said,
Here paske lombe rosted furþe was fette.
Thys lomb toke vp² cryst Ihesus,
A verry lombe slayn for vs,   84   [leaf 84, back, col. 2]

¹ *om.*   ² *vp* written over the line in MS.

4   MEDITATIONS ON THE

Christ cuts the lamb into small gobbets. As a servant He sits with them.
Alle yn smale gobettes he hyt kytte;
For vs as a scruau*n*t wyþ hem¹ he sytte,
W*ith* hem he² ete ry3t w*ith* glad chere,
And cunforted hem to ete yn fere,   88

But they are afraid.
But eue*r* þey dredde to ete gladlygh,
For sum sorowe semed hem nygh.
Whyles þey ete on þys manere,

Christ says, "I have desired to eat this Passover with you.
Cryst seyd þese wurdes dere:—   92
"Long haue y desyred w*ith* 3ow, y seye,
Þys paske to ete ar þat y deye:
Forsoþe, þe soþe ³to 3ow y³ seye,

One of you shall betray Me."
One of 3ow shal me betraye."   96
Byholde now, man, what sorowe and wo
Þe dycyplys toke⁴ to hem þo;

This word pierces their hearts.
Þys voys as a swerd here hertes pe*r*sed,
And to ete anone þey seced.   100

Each looks on other, and asks, "Lord, is it I?"
Eche loked on ouþe*r* w*ith* grysly ye,⁵
And seyd, "lorde wheþe*r* hyt be y⁶?"

Judas goes on eating.
Þe treytur ete faste, and wulde nat blyn,
As þogh þe⁷ tresu*n* come nat by hym.   104

John asks privily who should betray Him.
Pryuyly þan Ion to cryst gan prey,
And seyd, "lorde, who shal þe betrey?"
For specyal loue cryst hyt hym tolde,
"Iudas skaryot," he seyd, "beholde."   108
Þan Iohne þo3te hys herte wulde breste,

John lays his head on Christ's breast.
And leyd hys hede⁸ on crystys breste.
Ful mekely cryste lete hym lye stylle,
And suffred hy*m* do alle hys wylle.   112

Christ did not tell Peter.
Why cryst wulde nat to petyr telle,
Yn austyns sermou*n* þou mayst hyt spelle;⁹
3yf cryst þys treytur hym had tolde,
W*ith* nayles and teþ rent hym þey¹⁰ wulde.   116

What meekness to hold His disciple on His breast!
Byholde what mekenes yn hy*m* reste,
To holde hys dycyple so on hys brest.

¹ he*m*   ² *hem he* written over in MS.   ³⁻³ I. wil 3ow
⁴ toke*n*   ⁵ io   ⁶ I   ⁷ þat   ⁸ heuede
⁹ Homily on the Gospel for S. John's Day.   ¹⁰ he

A! how tendyrly þey loued yn fere,
Y[1] wys to loue, here mayst þou lere.   120
þenk, man, also a ruly poȝt,
What s[orow]e[2] hys dyscyplys ben yn broȝt.   [leaf 85]
At cry[stys][3] wurde, beholde, a none
þey etyn no more but madyn here mone;   124 The disciples cannot eat;
Eche[1] of hem loked vp-on[4] ouþer,
But cunseyl coude none take of ouþer. they know not what to counsel.
Beþenke, and holde þys weyl[5] yn þy mende,
How þys soper ys broȝt now to an ende.   128

The secunde poynt of the soper.

The secunde poynt, beþenke þe weyl,[6] The second point teaches meekness.
For grete mekenes hyt wyl þe spelle.
Whan þe soper was do, cryst ros anone, Supper is done;
And with hym þey ryse[7] vp euerychone;   132
To a logher place þey gunne þan to go, they go into a lower room.
þey þat þe hous haue sey seyn[8] ryȝt so.
He made hem sytte downe yn þat stede; Christ makes them sit.
Beholde, and[9] þenke weyl on crystys dede;   136
Hys cloþes he cast of swyþe sone,
Hys dycyplys wundred what he wulde done;
With a towel hym self he gert, He girds himself with a towel.
Watyr he badde brynge furþe smert,   140
He hyt yn a stonen bacyn put,
To wasshe here fete greued hym nat.[10] He washes their feet.
Petyr refused al þat seruyse; Peter refuses.
Cryst bad hym suffre on alle wyse.   144
Beholde now, man, eche doyng,
And þenke þys mekenes with grete wundryng, Think on the meekness of Christ.
That þe hygh mageste and myȝtyest eke,
Boweþ hym downe to a fysshers fete.   148
He stode krokyng,[11] on knees knelyng,
Afore hys cretures fete syttyng.

[1] I. [2] Illegible in MS., but sorowe in B. [3] Illegible in MS.
[4] fast vppon [5] e in weyl written over in MS. weil in B.
[6] welle [7] rese [8] seie, seiin [9] now and [10] not [11] croked

MEDITATIONS ON THE

A greater meekness yet: He does the same to Judas.

Wyþ hys handys hys¹ fete he wassheþ,
He wypeþ he cleppeþ,² and swetly³ kysseþ.   152
Of a more mekenes ȝyt mayst þou gryse,
þat he to hys treytur ⁴dyd þe same wyse.⁴
O Iudas, sore a shamed þou be may,
So meke and so⁵ myþe⁶ a mayster to tray;   156
þyn herte ys harder þan any hardnesse,
Aȝens swyche mekenes deþ for to dresse.

[leaf 85, col. 2]

They return to the place of supper.

Whan cryst þys seruyse had alle ydone,
To þe sopyng⁷ place aȝen þan þey come.   160
By þys ensample, and many ouþer,
He conforted⁸ hem to do to⁹ here broþer.

Think of the ensamples of meekness which Christ showed.

Man, here beþenke, yn eche degre,
How feyre ensample cryst shewed to þe;   164
Ensample of mekenes to þe he lete,
Whan he wysshe hys dyscyplys fete;
A grete ensample of mekenes¹⁰ loke,
Whan he hys flesshe to þy fode toke.   168
A feyre monasshyng hys sermoun shewed,

The learned should teach the "lewed."

þat þe lered men shulde teche þe lewed.
Pacyens he suffred,¹¹ hys treytur suffryng
So shamely to þe deþ, as a þef hym bryng;   172
Yn goyng to þe deþ, he shewed obedyens
Yn fulfyllyng¹² hys faders comoundemens.

Learn to pray, for He prayed thrice ere He was heard.

Stedfastly for to prey here mayst þou lere,
For he preyd fyrst þryys ar hys fadyr wulde here.
By þese vertues folue hym, y¹³ rede,   177
And yn to hys blys þey wyl þe lede.

The prydde poynt of þe soper.

The third point

The þryd poynt, man, haue yn mynde,¹⁴
How derwurly,¹⁵ afore hys ende,   180

---

¹ So in MS.; here in B. ² clippeþ ³ swetell hem
⁴—⁴ dede þis seruise ⁵ so written over in MS. ⁶ miþi
⁷ soupinge ⁸ cumfortede ⁹ to do to ¹⁰ charite ¹¹ shewed
¹² fulli-fillinge ¹³ I ¹⁴ mende ¹⁵ derwrþli

A derwurþ ȝyfte he wulde with þe lote,   *is the gift of Himself,*
Hym self al hole vn to þy mete.
Whan he hadde wasshe here al þer¹ fete,
And seten aȝen þere as þey ete,   184 *When He had sat down again,*
A newe testament he gan sone,
þe olde sacryfyce to fordone;
A new sacryfyce hym self he fonde,
And toke vp brede yn hys holy honde,   188 *He took bread,*
And to hys fadyr lyfte vpp hys ye,
He blessed and made hys precyus body;   *and gave it to His disciples, and said,*
To hys dycyplys he hyt ȝaue, and seyd,
"þys ys my body for ȝow betrayed."   192 *"This is my Body." Also the chalice, saying, "This is my Blood."*
Also of the chalys drynke he hem bad,
"þys ys my blode þat shal be shad."
Yn a memorand of hym with outyn ende,
He seyd, "makeþ þys yn my mende."   196 *[leaf 85, back]*
Beholde, how trewly and how deuoutly
He comunde and conforted þat blessed meyny.
þys mete shulde, most of any þyng,   *This meat shall gladden thy soul.*
Glade þy soule yn euery werchyng;   200
þyn herte shulde brenne for grete loue,
Whan þou hyt² takest to þy³ behoue;
No þyng more profytable, ne more chere,
þan hym self ⁴ne myȝt he⁴ leue here.   204
þat sacrament, þat þou seest þe before,   *The Sacrament was born of a maiden.*
Wundyrfully of a mayden was bore,
Fro heuene he lyȝte for þe to deye,   *Came down from heaven,*
He ros fro deþ to heuene to stye;   208 *Rose from death, and is now at God's right hand.*
On goddys ryȝt honde he ys syttyng;
He made heuene and erthe and alle þyng;
He gouerneþ alle þyng swetly and best,
He þat þou seest yn þe prestes fest,   212 *He that thou seest in the priest's hand,*
Yn whos powere onely hyt ys
To ȝyue⁵ þe blys,⁶ or endeles blys;

¹ þer   ² him   ³ þin   ⁴—⁴ he ne mighte
⁵ ȝeue   ⁶ So in MS., but *pine* in B.

MEDITATIONS ON THE

In the form of bread, is God's Son.

He þat þou seest, yn forme of brede,
Hyt ys goddys sone, quyk and¹ dede. 216
Wíth clene herte þou hym receyue,
For elles þy soule þou wylt deceyue.

The fourth point.

Þe fourþe poynt of þe soper.

The fourþe [point²] beholde and here,
A louesum lessun þou mayst lere. 220
Whan cryst hadde fed hem euerychone.

Christ began a sermon,

A feyre sermoun he began a none,
Ful of swetnes and ful of loue,
Ful of cumfort to oure behoue; 224

of which I take five parts.

Of whych wurdys sum mende to make,
Fyue pryncypals y þenke to take.

1st. He told them of His parting from them.

¶ The fyrst he tolde of hys partyng
And cumforted hem ful feyre, seyyng, 228
"ȝyt a whyle y am wíth ȝow now,
But faderles y wyl nat leue ȝow;
Y go and come to ȝow aȝen,
Forsoþe eftsones y wyl ȝow sen; 232

[leaf 85, back, col. 2]

Þan ȝoure hertys ioye shul make,
Þat ioye shal no man fro ȝow take."

His words cut them to the heart.

Lyke to þese mo gan he moue,
Þat kytte here hertys for grete loue. 236

2nd. He commanded them to love one another.

¶ In þe secunde þou mayst se
How he enformed hem yn charyte;
Ofte he reherced þese wurdes dere,
"Thys y ȝow hote, þat ȝe loue yn fere; 240
ȝyf ȝe loue alle men shul knowe þys,
Þat ȝe be my dere dyscyplys."
Þus hertly of charyte he tagħ hem well,
As þou shalt fynde yn Iones gospel. 244

3rd. He admonished them to keep His commandments.

¶ The prydde he tagħ hem by monasshyng
For to kepe hys comandyng:

¹ So in MS., but *nat* in B.   ² Not in MS., but in B.

SUPPER OF OUR LORD JESUS.

"Kepeþ my comandementys, ȝyf ȝe me loue,
ȝif ȝe hem kepe, ȝe dwelle in loue."[1] 248

¶ The fourþe, he warned hem feyþfullye,
What þey shulde suffre are þey shuld dye:
"Ȝe shul here haue sorowes some,
But truly y haue þys worlde ouercome, 252
And ȝyf þe worlde ȝow hate now,
Weteþ þat he me hated ar ȝow;
Ȝe shul be sorowful, þe wurlde shal ioye,
But ȝoure sorow shal turne to ioye." 256

¶ The fyueþe, beþenke how cryst Ihesus
To hys fadyr turned and preyd for vs.
"Fadyr, kepe hem whyche þou ȝaue me,
For whyle y was with hem y kepte hem to þe; 260
Now, holy fadyr, to þe y come,
For hem y pray, and nat for þys wone;
And nat onely for hem, but for alle men
þat shul byleue yn me by hem. 264
Fadyr, y wyl where þat y be
þey be with me, my blysse to se."
Þese wurdys, and ouþer þat hem[2] tolde,
Kytte here hertys and made hem colde. 268
Beholde now þe dyscyplys yn here mornyng,[3]
How þey stonde alle heuy here hedys bowyng,
Mornyng,[3] sorowyng, and ofte syghyng,
Þat cryst wytnessed to hem seyyng, 272
"For y þese wurdes to ȝow haue seyd,
Sorwe ȝoure hertes haþ alle be leyd."
Byholde how homely Ion lyþ slepyng
On crystys brest, as hys derlyng. 276
Þys sermoun at crystys[4] brest slepyng he soke,
And toke hyt to vs yn holy boke,
Among al ouþer as cryst tagh hem.
He seyd, "aryseþ and go we hen." 280

4th. He warned them of the sufferings they should undergo.

5th. He prayed to His Father

for them and for all men.

"Father, I will that where I am they may be with me."

The disciples all stand sighing.

[leaf 86]

Behold how "homely" John lies on Christ's breast!

Christ says, "Arise, go we hence."

---

[1] Line 248 is supplied from B.   [2] he hem in B.
[3] moreninge   [4] his. *crystys* written over in MS.

> A! what drede went yn hem þo,
> þey wyst nat whedyr for to go,
> For þey went, as y shal sey;
> Cryst endyd hys sermoun by þe wey. 284

As they go the disciples are like chickens creeping under the hen's wing,

> Behold þe dyscyplys, yn here wendyng,
> As chekenes[1] crepyn vndyr þe dame wyng;
> Some go byfore, and some go behynde,
> Hys blessed wurdes to haue yn mynde; 288
> One þrest on hym, eftsones anoþer,
> þat meke mayster ys neuer þe wroþer.

They go over the brook Cedron,

> Fast þey went, and come a none,
> Ouer a broke men callen Cedron. 292

where Judas awaits them.

> Hys treytur he abode þere tyl he come,
> And ouþer armed men, a grete summe.
> Now foleweþ, yn þys medytacyun,
> To trete of crystys passyun. 296

Here begynneþ þe passyun.

Prepare your heart to bleed!

> Now crystyn creature, take goode hede,
> And do þyn herte for pyte to blede;
> Loþe þou nat hys sorowes to se,
> þe whych hym loþed nat to suffre for þe. 300
> Beholde and þenke with ruly mone

What pains He suffers!

> What peynes he suffred ar morowe none;
> Beholde hym yn an orcherd syttyng,
> Hys treytur þere mekely abydyng; 304

He bids His disciples watch,

> He byt hys dyscyplys pray and wake,
> þat none temptacyun ȝow ouertake;

and goes from them a stone's cast,

> A stones kast þan from hem he went,
> And to hys dere fadyr hys knees he bent. 308

[leaf 86, col. 2]

and prays,

> Now þenke how mekely and how reuerently,
> To hys swete fadyr he preyeþ an[2] hy:—

"My Father, hear my prayer and despise it not.

> "My wurschypful fadyr, y pray to þe,
> Bowe þyn eres and lestene to me, 312

[1] The second *e* written over in MS.   [2] on

PASSION OF OUR LORD JESUS.

Here my bone and dyspyse hyt noȝt,
For sorowe my soule haþ ȝow soȝt;
My spyryt ys anguyssed ful sore yn me, — My spirit is anguished.
Myn herte ys dysturbled, fadyr, now se; 316
þou sentest me hedyr, as þy wyl ys, — Thou sentest me.
To bye mankynde aȝen to blys;
To do þy wyl, y seyd y go; — I said, To do Thy will, I go.
Yn þe bokes hede hyt ys wryte so; 320
Here haue y be and preched þyn helþe, — Here have I preached Thine health.
Yn pouert, yn trauayle & noþyng yn welþe:
Fadyr, þyn hestes y haue fulfylt, — I have fulfilled Thine 'hests.'
And more y wyl, ȝyf þou wylt; 324
þou seest what sorowe ys to me dyȝt, — Thou seest my sorrow.
Of my foos aȝens alle ryȝt,
Ȝyf any wykkednes ys yn me founde, — If any wickedness is found in me,
Or euyl for euyl haue ȝyue[1] astounde, 328 then am I worthy of these pains.
þan were y wurþy þese peynes to fong;
But, fadyr, þou wost weyl þey do me wrong; — Father, Thou knowest they wrong me,
Euyl for gode þey haue me ȝoue,
And also grete hate for my loue. 332 and give me hate for love.
My dyscyple, whych y haue chersed,[2]
Me to betraye hym haue þey hyred; — They have hired my disciple to betray me.
At þrytty pens my mede ys take,
þey haue me preysed my wo to awake; 336
My swete fadyr, y prey to þe, — My Father, rise up to help me.
Ryse vp redyly yn helpe of me,
For þogh þey wyte[3] nat þat y am þy sone, — They know not that I am Thy Son.
Ȝyt, by cause þat y here wone, 340
Lyuyng with hem Innocent lyfe,
þey shulde nat shape me so grete stryfe.
Þenk[4] þat y stode afore þy syȝt, — Think that I stand before Thee
To speke for hem boþe gode and ryȝt, 344
To turne a waye [5]from hem, fadyr,[5] þy mode,[6] — to turn away Thy wrath from them,
But wheþer nat euyl be ȝulde for gode;

[1] ȝulde [2] chershed [3] wete [4] Thenke fader
[5—5] fader from hem [6] wraþþe written over mode in B.

12   MEDITATIONS ON THE

[leaf 86, back]

  For þey to my soule deluyn a lake,
  A vyleynys deþ to me þey shape; 348

Dear Father, let this death go from me;
  Wharfore, dere fadyr, ȝyf hyt mow be,
  Y prey þat þys deþ mow go fro me;

If not, Thy will be done.
  Ȝyf þou se hyt be nat so best,
  Þy wyl be ydo, ryȝt as þou lest. 352

I commend myself unto Thee."
  But, fadyr, myn herte y betake þe,
  Kepe hyt and strenþe hyt how so hyt be."
  To hys dyscyplys hys wey¹ þan he toke,

He finds His disciples sleeping.
  He fond hem slepyng and hem sone awoke:² 356
  Here yen³ were slepy and heuy as clay,
  He bad hem algates wake and pray.

He prays twice, thrice, the same orison.
  Aȝen to pray he toke hys pas,
  Twyys, þryys, yn dyuers place. 360
  Þe same orysun þat he preyd byfore,
  He preyd now and ded to more:

"Father, I am here to do Thy will.
  "Fadyr, ȝyf þys deþ mow nat fro me go,
  Y am here, þy wyl be algates do. 364

I commend my mother and brethren unto Thee."
  My swete modyr, fadyr, y þe betake,
  My breþren also, kepe hem fro wrake;
  Y kepte hem þyrwhylys y⁴ was with hem,
  My derwurþe fadyr, now kepe þou þem." 368
  Þus long he preyd tyl þat he wax hote,

For anguish His blood ran down as sweat.
  For anguys hys blode ran down ryȝt as swote.
  Man, take ensample here at goddes sone,
  Whan þou shalt pray of god any bone, 372
  Prey so stedfastly tyl þat þou be herde,
  For cryst preyd þryes ar þat he were herd.

While He prayed
  Whyles he þus preyd yn grete dolour

S. Michael came and said,
  Seynt myghel lyȝt a down fro heuene toure, 376
  And hym cumforted and seyd þus:

"All haill! Thy prayer and bloody sweat I have offered to thy Father."
  "Alheyl, my lorde, cryst Ihesus!
  Þy preyer and þy swote blody
  Y haue offred to þy fadyr an hy, 380
  Yn syȝte of alle þe courte of heuene;

¹ wei ² he woke ³ eien ⁴ þat I.

For ʒow we preyd alle wit h o steuene,
þat he shuld nat suffre þe dey¹ þus;
by fadyr, by resun, answered vs,   384   He answered,
'My derwurþe sone wote þys ful weyl,   [leaf 86, back, col. 2]
þat mannes soule, þat lyþ yn helle,   "My Son knows if He will
May nat semely to blys be broʒt,   save souls He must die."
But þey wit h hys blode be fyrst oute boʒt.   388
þarfore, ʒyf my sone wyl soules saue,
Nedes he mote for hem þe deþ haue.'"
þan cryst answered, wit h mylde state: Christ said,
"Soules saluatyun y wyl algate,   392   "I choose death;
þarfore to dey raþer y chese,
þan we þe soules yn helle shulde lese,
þe whych my fadyr formed to hys lykenes:
Hys wyl be ydo, y wyll no lesse."   396   His will be done."
þan seyd þe aungel to hym an hy: The Angel said,
"Cumforte þe weyl and do manly;   "Comfort thyself and do manly.
Hyt ys semely to hym þat ys hyghest,
Grete þynges to do, and suffre mest;   400
by pyne shal sone be ouerpaste,
And ioye shal sewe euer for to last;
by fadyr seyþ euer wit h þe he ys,   Thy Father is ever with Thee."
by modyr he kepeþ and þy dyscyplys."   404
Cryst bade þe aungel, "go, grete þou² me
To my fadyr dere an hy yn hys cyte."
Beholde now, how mekely þys cumforte he toke
Of hys owne creature, as seyþ þe boke,   408
A lytyl from aungels he ys made lesse,   He was made little less than the angels.
Whyl he ys yn þys valey of dyrknes;
þys wo he suffred yn hys manhede,   He suffered in His manhood,
But god suffred naght³ yn hys god hede.   412   not in His God-head.
þe þryd tyme he ros from hys preyour
All be sprunge wit h blody couloure;
Beholde hym auysyly, þan shalt þou se
Wit h oute grete dolour þys may nat be   416

¹ dele   ² þou written over in MS.   ³ noght

He returns to His disciples.	To hys dyscyplys went he, and seyd,	
	"He cumþ ny þat haþ me betrayd."	
Judas comes, and says,	Anone come Iudas, with hys cumpanye,	
	Cryst went aȝens hym ful myldely :	420
"Hail, Master!"	"Heyl, mayster !" he seyd, and to hym sterte,	
	He kessed hys mouþe with tresun yn herte.	
[leaf 87] They all fall upon Him.	þo fyl vpp on hym alle þe touþer route,	
	For erst of knowlechyng þey were yn doute.	424
	þe cursed houndes runne hym aboute,	
	And drowe hym furþe, now yn, now oute ;	
Some bind, some blind, some spit upon, some buffet, some scorn Him.	Sum bynte hym, sum blyndyþ hym, & sum on hym spyt,	
	Sum boffeteþ hym, and sum seyþ, "telle who þe smyt ;"	
	Sum scorneþ hym, and sum syngeþ of hym a song,	429
	Some axen questyons, to[1] do hym wrong ;	
He says nothing.	But to hem no þyng answere he wulde.	
	Werse þo þan a fole of hem [2]he ys[2] holde,	432
"Where is Thy wisdom?"	Some seyd, "where ys now all þy wysdom ?	
	þou held þe wyser þan any ouþer man ;	
	Of oure patryarkes & prestes þou haddest despyte,	
"Thou shalt die."	þarefor [3]þou shalt[3] haue of vs þe deþ astyte ;	436
"If Thou art God's Son, help Thyself."	Thou seyst þat þou art goddes sone,	
	Helpe þy self[4] ȝyf þou kone."	
Some seek false witness.	Sum seke aȝens hym fals wytnes,	
	Sum seyn on hym vnsekernes,	440
	Some tugge,[5] sum drawe[6] fro ce to ce,[7]	
Ah, how may this be!	A! lorde Ihesu, how may þys be ?	
	þyrwhylys he suffred þys[8] sorow & wo,	
The disciples run away.	Hys dyscyplys runne awey hym fro.	444
	To maudelens hous Ion went ful ryȝt,	
	þere as þe soper was made þeke nyȝt ;	
John tells Our Lady of her Son's punishment.	Oure lady he tolde and here felawshepe	
	Of here dere sonys shenshepe.	448
	þenk, man, of þe dyscyplys doyng!	

[1] for to. *to* written over in MS.   [2-2] is he   [3-3] shalt þou
[4] þeself now   [5] tugge him   [6] drawe him
[7] *place* written over *ce to ce* in MS.   [8] om.

Þey wepe, þey weyle, here handys þey wryng,
Here mayster ys take, þat shulde hem kepe;
Þey renne aboute as herdles shepe. 452
Oure lady wente here seluyn alone, *She goes alone to pray.*
To þe fadyr of heuene she made þys mone:—
"My wurschypfullest fadyr, and moste meke, *"My Father, my sweet Son*
Moste mercyable, and most helpyng eke, 456 *I commend to Thee.*
My swete sone y ȝow betake!
Derwurþe fadyr, kepeþ hym fro wrake, *Keep Him from 'wrack.'*
Beþ nat cruel to my dere chylde,
For to alle men ȝe are ful mylde. 460
Fadyr, shal my chylde be dede, Ihesus, [leaf 87, col. 2] *Shall He die?*
What haþ he mysdo to dey þus?
But, fadyr, ȝyf ȝe wyl mankynde *Father, if Thou wilt save mankind,*
Be boȝt to blys wiþoutyn ende, 464
Y prey outher wyse doþ bye¹ hem now, *do it in some other manner.*
For al þyng ys posyble to ȝow.
Lateþ nat, fadyr, my sone dede be; *Let not my Son die.*
Y pray ȝow ȝeldeþ hym aȝen to me; 468
He ys so buxum to do ȝoure wyl,
Þat he nat chargeþ hym self to spyl.
Helpeþ my sone fro cursed houndes; *Help Him from cursed hounds."*
Dere fadyr, bryngeþ hym out from here hondes." 472
Þenke, man, now & rewe on here syghyng,
For þys preyd she wiþ watyr wepyng.

The medytacyun of þe oure of pryme.

On a colde mornyng, at pryme of daye, *The priests prepare themselves.*
The prestes and prynces gun² hem araye; 476
Both bollers of wyne and eche agadlyng *Drunkards come to see Jesus.*
Come oute for to se of Ihesus endyng.
Þey shokyn hym ³oute þan³ of hys cloþyng, *They strip Him,*
And bonden hys handys fast hym behynd, 480
As a þefe among hem⁴ led furþe he was, *lead Him to Pilate, thence to Herod and Caiaphas.*
Now to pylat, now to eroud, now to kayphas.

¹ bie ² gunne ³⁻³ þan out ⁴ hem written over in MS.
MEDITATIONS. 3

16 MEDITATIONS ON THE

<table>
<tr><td></td><td>þey cryde, "þou þefe, come to þy dome!"</td><td></td></tr>
<tr><td></td><td>And he, as a meke lambe, aftyr hem come.</td><td>484</td></tr>
<tr><td>His Mother goes to meet Him.</td><td>Hys modyr, Ion, and[1] ouþer kyn,</td><td></td></tr>
<tr><td></td><td>Wente by a bypaþ to mete with hym.</td><td></td></tr>
<tr><td></td><td>When þey hym saye so shamely ylad,</td><td></td></tr>
<tr><td></td><td>No tunge may telle what sorowe þey had.</td><td>488</td></tr>
<tr><td></td><td>þenke, whan hys modyr fyrst hym byhelde,</td><td></td></tr>
<tr><td>She swoons in the field.</td><td>Aswo[2] she fyl down yn þe felde:</td><td></td></tr>
<tr><td></td><td>þan cryst was turmented yn moste kare,</td><td></td></tr>
<tr><td></td><td>Whan he say hys modyr so pytusly fare.</td><td>492</td></tr>
<tr><td></td><td>Beholde to pylat he ys furþe drawe,</td><td></td></tr>
<tr><td>He is falsely accused. Pilate sends Him to Herod.</td><td>Falsly acused aȝens here lawe:</td><td></td></tr>
<tr><td></td><td>Pylat sent hym to eroude þe kyng,</td><td></td></tr>
<tr><td></td><td>And eroude þe kyng was glad of hys comyng;</td><td>496</td></tr>
<tr><td></td><td>A myracle he coueyted of hym for to se,</td><td></td></tr>
<tr><td>[leaf 87, back]</td><td>But noþer myracle ne wurde hym shewe wulde he.</td><td></td></tr>
<tr><td></td><td>þan as a fole eroude hym hadde,</td><td></td></tr>
<tr><td>Herod clothes Him with a white cloth, and sends Him again to Pilate.</td><td>And with a whyte cloþe y[3] skorne hym he clad,</td><td>500</td></tr>
<tr><td></td><td>And sente hym aȝen to syre pylate:</td><td></td></tr>
<tr><td></td><td>And þo was made frenshepe þar arst was debate.</td><td></td></tr>
<tr><td></td><td>Nat onely a mysdoer now [4]he ys[4] holde,</td><td></td></tr>
<tr><td></td><td>But as a lewed fole he ys eke tolde:</td><td>504</td></tr>
<tr><td></td><td>þey cryed on hym, as foules on owle,</td><td></td></tr>
<tr><td>With wet and dirt they defile Him.</td><td>With wete and eke dung þey hym defoule.</td><td></td></tr>
<tr><td></td><td>Hys modyr þat tyme folwed hym longe,</td><td></td></tr>
<tr><td></td><td>And wundred þat he wulde suffre swyche wrong.</td><td>508</td></tr>
<tr><td></td><td>þey broȝt hym to pylate, he stode ful feynt;</td><td></td></tr>
<tr><td></td><td>Boldely þe[5] howndes pursewed here pleynt.</td><td></td></tr>
<tr><td></td><td>Pylate þoȝt to delyuer hym,</td><td></td></tr>
<tr><td></td><td>For no cause of deþ he fonde yn hym:</td><td>512</td></tr>
<tr><td>"Scourge Him, and let Him go."</td><td>"Y wyl vndyr neme hym, he seyd þo,</td><td></td></tr>
<tr><td></td><td>Do scurge hym weyl, and so late hym go."</td><td></td></tr>
<tr><td>They bind Him to a pillar.</td><td>To a pylour fast þan þey hym bownde,</td><td></td></tr>
<tr><td></td><td>þey bette hym, & rent hym, wounde be[6] wounde.</td><td>516</td></tr>
</table>

[1] *and* his   [2] Aswowe   [3] *in*   [4]—[4] is he
[5] þo   [6] *om*.

Beholde now, man, a ruly¹ syȝt! *A rueful sight.*
þy cumly kyng stant bounde vpryȝt,
Alle forwounded for þe yn² mode;
Beholde how he wadeþ yn hys owne blode! 520
ȝyt þey bete hym and leyn³ on sore, *They lay on until they are weary.*
Tyl þey be wery and mow no more.
þe pyler⁴ þat þey hym to bow[n]den⁵ *The pillar shows the blood now.*
ȝyt sheweþ þe blode of hys woundyn. 524
A, lorde Ihesu! how may þys be?
Ho was so hardy þat spoyled þe?
Ho more hardy þat þe bounden?
Ho moste hardy þat þe wounden? 528
Almyȝty god! where art þou now? *Almighty God, where art Thou?*
þese houndes seme myȝtyer þan þou!
But trewly, þou sone of ryȝtwysnes,
Withdrawest þy bemes ouer oure derkenes. 532
Whan þey hadde bete hym þus pytusly,
þey broȝt hym to pylate, & cryed an⁶ hy,
"Syre, þys fole kalleþ⁷ hym self a kyng! *"This fool calleth Himself a king!*
Cloþe we hym þarfore yn kynges cloþyng." 536 *[leaf 87, back, col. 2] Clothe we Him in king's clothing!"*
þenk þys was y do at þe oure of pryme:
þe dowyng of⁸ þred now wyl y ryme.

The medytacyun of þe predde oure.

Wyþ purpyl þey cloþed hym alle yn skorne, *They clothe Him with purple.*
 And syþen ⁹krounde hym with a croune⁹ of [þorne;
Yn hys hand a rede dyd þey take, *In His hand they put a reed.*
And manyone on hys hede þey brake;
þey sette hym opunly yn here seyng,
And knelyd, and seyd,¹⁰ "heyl, syre kyng!" 544 *"Hail, Sir king!"*
A Ihesu! þy pacyens may nat be tolde.
þou angry man, þy sauyour here beholde;
For þe he suffred þys pyne, fys shame,
And for a¹¹ lytyl wurde þou wylt men grame. 548

¹ rewli ² wiþ ³ leien ⁴ peler ⁵ bownden ⁶ on
⁷ kalled ⁸ of þe ⁹⁻⁹ corownde wiþ corowne: *croûne* in MS.
 ¹⁰ cride ¹¹ o

"Crucify Him! Crucify Him!"

Pilate condemns Him.

The hounds lead Him out at once.

A cross is fetched,

and put on His shoulders.

They hurry Him.

[leaf 8ʙ]

Yet more shame!

Thieves are his companions.

The prophecy must needs be fulfilled.

Eftsones to pylate þey come cryyng,
And seyd, "syre, saue Cesar, we haue no kyng;
Who hym self a kyng wyl make
By lawe þe deþ he most take." 552
Tho seyd pylat, "what wyl ȝe wíth hym?"
Þey cryed, [1]"crucyfye, crucyfye[1] hym!"
Pylat þan dredde for þe peples voys,
And dampnede hys lorde to dye on þe croys. 556
Ha, fals Iustyce! where fynst þou þat resun,
So for to dampne an ynnocent man?[2]
Whan he was dampned on cros for to hong,
Þe houndes wulde not tary hym long, 560
But anone from pylat þey led[3] hym oute,
And ioed[4] þat here malys was broȝt aboute.
A cros [5]was fet furþ,[5] boþe long and grete,
Þe lengþe þerof was fyftene fote. 564
Vp on hys shulder þys cros þey kast,
Þat hys bak bent and wel ny to braste;
Þey punged hym furþe þurgh euery slogh,
As an hors ys prykked þat goþ yn[6] plogh. 568
Beholde now, man, wíth wepyng herte,
And late nat þy þoȝt lyȝtly a sterte.
Cryst goþ krokedly þys heuy cros vndyr,
And feyntly hyt bereþ, hyt ys no wundyr. 572
Þey hye hym, and ho goþ wíthoutyn any stryfe,
And bereþ hys owne deþ, and bereþ þy lyfe.
Ȝyt hym ys shape more shame and shenshepe;
Þeuys be[7] broȝt to hym yn hys felawshepe! 576
Ȝyt more, for cryste bereþ hys owne, Iuwyse,
Y fynde nat þat þe þeues ded [8]þe same[8] wyse.
A, Ihesu! what shame þey do to ȝow here,
To make ȝow so vyleynsly[9] þese þeues fere. 580
But nedys þe prophecye mot be fulfylled,

[1–1] crucifige, crucifige: in the MS. is a mark over the final *e* which may be a very small *g*—*orucyfyge*.
[2] moun [3] ledden [4] ioide [5–5] furþ was fet
[6] in þe [7] ben [8–9] on þat [9] vilensli

PASSION OF OUR LORD JESUS.

þat seyd,¹ with wykked men he ys spylled.	Isa. 53, 9.
Mary hys modyr folewed a ver,	Mary follows,
She myȝt for pres come hym no ner ; 584	
A shorter wey for to chese þan bygan she,	
To mete with here swete sone withoute the cyte ;	
And þo she say² hym þat grete tre bere,	
Half dede she wax and swouned ³ryȝt þare ;³ 588	and swoons again
Ful feyne she wulde hys peynes alyþed ;	
She myȝt nat, so þese houndes hym hyed.	
None of hem myȝt speke ouþer to,	
For sorowe þat eche had of ouþer þo. 592	
Furþe þey dryuen hym with hys berdoun,	They drive Him till He faints.
Tyl he for feyntnesse fyl ny adoun.	
For ouer long tyme þat cros he bare,	
þe place weyl shewyþ, who so haþ be þare. 596	
Thos howndes were lothe hys deþ for to tarye,	
þey dredyn þat pylat hys dome wulde varye,	They are afraid Pilate will change his mind.
For euer hyt semed by hys wylle,	
þat he was loþ Ihesu to spylle. 600	
A man þey mette, and hym areyned,	They meet a man and lay the cross on him.
To bere þe cros þey hym constreyned ;	
So furþe as a þefe, Ihesu þey nam,	
Tyl þey to þe mounte of caluarye cam. 604	

The medytacyun of⁴ syxte oure of⁵ none.

Thenk now, man, how hyt ys down	Think,
Yn þe oure of⁴ syxte of⁵ none.	
Beholde þe peynes of þy sauyour,	
And crucyfye þyn herte with grete dolour. 608	and crucify thine heart.
Whan he to caluarye mounte was broȝt,⁶	
Beholde what werkmen þere wykkedly wroȝt :	[leaf 88, col. 2]
Some dyggen, sum deluyn, sum erþe oute⁷ kast,	
Some pycchen þe cros yn þe erþe fast ; 612	They pitch the cross.
On euery syde sum laddres vpp sette,	Ladders are set up.
Sum renne aftyr hamers, some nayles fette ;	

¹ seiþ ² sagh ³⁻³ þere ⁴ of þe ⁵ and of ⁶ ibroght ⁷ vp

	Some dyspoyle hym oute dyspetusly,	
	Hys cloþys cleuyn on hys swete body;	616
His clothes are rent off.	þey rente hem of as þey were wode:	
	Hys body aȝen ran alle on blode.	
	A! wit*h* what sorow hys modyr was fedde,	
	Whan she say¹ hy*m* so naked and alle bled!²	620
	Fyrþer more, þan gan she to seche,	
	And say þat þey had left hym no breche.	
	She ran þan³ þurgh hem, and hastyly hyde,	
Mary wraps kerchiefs round Him.	And wi*th* here kercheues hys hepys she wryde.	624
	She wulde do⁴ more, but she ne myȝt,	
	For fersly here swete⁵ sone ys from her plyȝt.	
They draw Him to the cross-foot.	To þe cros fote þey drowe hym hyyng.	
	Se now þe maner of crucyfyyng.	628
Ladders are raised.	Twey laddres ben sette þe cros behynde,	
	Twey enmyes on hem smartly gu*n* glymbe,⁶	
	Wi*th* hamers and nayles sharply whet:	
	A shorte⁷ ladder before was fet.⁸	632
	þere as þe fete shorte⁷ weren,	
	Beholde þys syȝte wi*th* ruly teren,	
Christ goes up without urging,	Cryst Ih*es*u hys body vpp stey,	
	By þat short ladder, þat cros an hy;	636
	Wi*th*oute ȝenseyyng he gan vp wende,	
	And whan he com to þe laddres ende,	
	Toward þe cros hys bak he layde,	
and extends His arms.	And hys real armes oute he dysplayde;	640
	Hys fayre handys oute he streyȝte,	
	And to þe crucyfyers oute⁹ he reyȝte;	
He lifts His eyes and says, "Here am I, Father;	And to hys fadyr he kast¹⁰ hys yen,¹¹	
	And seyd, "here am y,¹² fadyr myn:	644
	Vnto þys cros þou mekest me,	
I offer myself for mankind:	Me for mankynde y offre to þe;	
	My breþren and sustryn þou hast made hem;	
[leaf 88, back]	For my loue, fadyr, beþ¹³ mercyable to hem;	648

¹ sagh   ² bebled   ³ þo   ⁴ ha do   ⁵ *om.*   ⁶ climbe
⁷ shorter   ⁸ So in MS; but *set* in B.   ⁹ hom   ¹⁰ caste
¹¹ ein   ¹² I. am   ¹³ be

Alle olde syn*n*es þou hem forȝyue,
And graun*t*e hem blys w*ith* vs for to lyue :
Derwurþe fadyr, saue alle mankyn*n*e,
Lo here y am offred for here synne."   652
Whyle he þus preyd[1] yn hys herte,
The too Iew a nayle yn hys hand gerte,
þe touþ*er* þey drowe tyl þe veynes braste,
And nayled þe touþ*er* [2]hand þ*er* fyne[2] faste.   656
Anone þey com down w*ith* alle here gere,
And alle þe laddres þan remouede were.
Beholde, man, now a grete[3] angwys !
For by þe armes hys body alle hangys.   660
To hys fete anone þan þey straked,
þey haled he*m* harde, tyl þe cros kraked ;
Alle þe ioyntes þan brasto*n* atwynne.
A, Ihe*s*u ! why suffrest þou[4] þus for oure syn*n*e !   664
Hys fete þey nayled as tree to lede ;
þan myȝt [5]nat he[5] moue more but hys hede.
Beholde þese nayles beren alle hys lemes,
Loke, alle aboute hy*m* renne blody stremes.   668
He suffred sorowes byttyr and fele,
Mo þan any tunge may rede or telle.
Betwene þeues tweyn þey hange hy*m* y*n* samen,
A, what wrong, what peyne, & also what shame*n*!   672
Some dyspyseþ hys lore, and seyþ,
" Fy ! þat goddes temple dystroyþ ! "
Sum seyþ, " saue þy selfe, ȝyf þou kun*n*e ;[6]
Com adowne, ȝyf þou be goddes sone."   676
Also þe Iewes, þat crucyfyed hym,
þe cloþes of hym þey parted[7] atwyn*n*e.
Su*m* seyd, "ouþ*er* coude he weyl saue,
But now hym owne self[8] may he nat saue."   680
þus whyl hys modyr þe cros stant nye,

Side notes:
be merciful unto them."
They nail Him to the cross.
Behold His anguish.
He can only move His head.
Bloody streams run all about Him.
"Fy, Thou that destroyest the Temple!
Come down, if Thou be God's Son."
"He could save others, Himself He cannot save."

---

[1] stilli preide   [2]–[2] hon*d*e þer*e* fin   [3] *a grete a grete* in MS.
[4] þou   [5]–[5] he nat   [6] kone   [7] parteden
[8] *hymon*neself* in MSS.

His mother stands near.	Ruly on here sone she kast here ye.¹	
	A! here sorow, here angwys, here pyne,²	
	Y may sum þenk, but nat alle seyn;	684
	Truly yn herte she ys crucyfyed,	
[leaf 88, bk, col. 2]	Ful feyn for sorow she wulde ha deyd.	
	Here sones peyne was eke moche þe more,	
	Þat he here peynes say³ be so sore;	688
He complains,	And to hys fadyr stylly he pleynes:	
"Father, seest Thou not my Mother?	"Fadyr! seest þou nat my modyr peynes?	
	On þys cros she ys with me,	
I should be crucified, not she."	Y shulde be crucyfyed, and nat she;	692
	My crucyfyyng suffyseþ for alle mankynne,	
	For now y bere alle here synne;	
	Yn to þy kepyng y here betake,	
	Derwurþe fadyr, here peynes⁴ þou slake."	696
Also she prayed,	Also she preyde, with byttyr wepyng,	
"My Father, shall my dear Son die?"	And seyd, "my fadyr, euer lastyng,	
	Shal my dere sone deye algate?	
	Hym now for to saue me þenkeþ to late.	700
	Se, fadyr, what angwys now yn hym ys,	
	Y prey þe sumdele hys peyne þou lys."	
By her stand John, the three Maries, James, Magdalene, and Cleophas [*Salome* in Lat. orig.].	By here stant Iohne, and maryes þre,	
	Iacobe, maudeleyn, and cleophe.	704
	Wundyr ys to telle what sorowe þey make,	
	For here swete mayster ys from hem take.	

𝕿𝖍𝖊 𝖒𝖊𝖉𝖞𝖙𝖆𝖈𝖞𝖚𝖓 𝖔𝖋 𝖙𝖍𝖊 𝖜𝖚𝖗𝖉𝖞𝖘 𝖕𝖆𝖙 𝖈𝖗𝖞𝖘𝖙 𝖘𝖕𝖆𝖐 𝖍𝖆𝖓𝖌𝖞𝖓𝖌 𝖚𝖕𝖕 𝖔𝖓 𝖕𝖊 𝖈𝖗𝖔𝖘.

Christ speaks seven words.	Thenk how⁵ cryst, hongyng on þe cros,⁶	
	Seuene [wur]dys [seide⁷] with ful ruly voys.	708
	Þe fyrst wurde þat he þere hongyng seyd,	
	For hys crucyfyers mekely he preyd,	
1. "Father, forgive them,	"Fadyr, forȝyue hem here synnes sone,	

¹ eye ² pein ³ sagh ⁴ peine ⁵ now how
⁶ crois ⁷ not in MS.; *seide* in B.

"SEVEN WORDS" OF JESUS CHRIST.

For þey[1] wyte[2] nat wel what þey done."   712   they know not what they do."
Grete loue, grete pacyens, þys wurde shewyþ þe,
þat þou shust pray for hem þat þy foos be.
Þe secunde wurde to hys modyr was mone :[3]
"Womman," he[4] seyd, "beholde þy sone."   716   2. "Woman, behold thy son."
To hys dyscyple he seyd a nouþer,
And seyd, "beholde þy modyr, broþer."   "Behold thy mother, brother."
He wulde nat marye hys modyr clepe,
Lest for grete loue here herte wulde breke.   720
Þe þred to þe þefe,—"forsoþe y seye þe,
To day yn blys þou shalt be *with* me."—   [leaf 89]
Þe fourþe he cryed wyþ voys an hy,   3. "To-day shalt thou be in bliss with me."
"Eli, Eli, lamaȝabatany!"[5]   724
Þat ys, my god, my god, wharto   4. "My God, My God,
Hast þou forsake me yn my wo!   why hast thou forsaken me?"
As who seyþ, þou me forsakest,
And for þys wurlde to day me betakest.   728
Þe fyþe[6] wurde he seyd, "y þryste :"   5. "I thirst."
Þan þe houndes wroȝtyn werste.
Þey þoȝte to noye hym moste of alle,
And ȝaue hym to drynke aysel and galle.   732   They give Him gall.
He tastede sumdele hys þryst for to lyne :[7]
A! A! how strong was þat[8] pyne.
Þogh yt he expouñed yn a sermoun,
Þat he þrysted soulys saluacyun,   736
Ȝyt truly þe manhede þrysted on þe[9] rode,
For he was ful drye for faute of blode.
The syxte wurde anone he spellede,
And seyd, "alle þyng ys now fulfylled."   740   6. "All things are now fulfilled."
As who seyþ, fadyr, fulfylled y haue
Alle þyn hestys, þy soules to saue :
Y haue be skurged, scorned, dyffyed,
Wounded, angred, and crucyfyed ;   744

[1] þey written over in MS.   [2] wete   [3] nome
[4] *ho* written over in MS.   [5] lama sabatani   [6] fifþe
[7] B has the gloss *slake*.   [8] þan his   [9] *om*.

MEDITATIONS ON THE

<ul style="list-style:none">
<li>Fulfylled y haue þat wrytyn ys of me,</li>
<li>þarfore, dere fadyr, take¹ me to þe.</li>
<li>Ʒyf þou wylt more, y wyl hyt fulfylle,</li>
<li>For here now y hange to do þy wylle.   748</li>
</ul>

His Father said,
"Come to my bliss;

<ul style="list-style:none">
<li>þan seyd hys fadyr, my derwurþe sone,</li>
<li>Com to þy blys þere euer to wone;</li>
<li>Alle þyng fulweyl þou hast fulfylled,</li>
</ul>

I will no more;

Y wyl no more þat þou be þus spylled,   752

souls thou hast brought from bond; come, sit on my right hand."

<ul style="list-style:none">
<li>For soules þou haste² broʒt oute of bonde,</li>
<li>Come sone and sytte on my ryʒt honde.</li>
<li>Anone he traueyled as men done þat dyen,</li>
<li>Now shyttyng,³ now kastyng vpward, hys yen,   756</li>
<li>þrowyng hys hede,⁴ now here, now þore,</li>
<li>For bodely strengþe haþ he no more;</li>
<li>þe seuenþe wurde ful loude þan he spake:</li>
</ul>

[leaf 89, col. 2]
7. "Father, into thy hands I commend my spirit."

<ul style="list-style:none">
<li>"Fadyr, yn þyn handys my spyryt y betake."   760</li>
<li>He ʒelde vp hys goste, hys fadyr þankyng,</li>
<li>Toward hys brest hys hede⁴ hangyng.</li>
<li>þan to þat crye Centuryo turned sone,</li>
<li>And seyde, "forsoþe þys was goddys sone."   764</li>
<li>For wyþ þat grete crye þe goste gan furþe go:</li>
<li>Ouþer men⁵ whan þey deye do nat so.</li>
</ul>

This cry is heard in hell by those

<ul style="list-style:none">
<li>þat crye was so grete, as y þe telle,</li>
<li>þat hyt was weyl herde downe yn to helle.   768</li>
<li>þenk now, man, what ioye þere ys</li>
<li>Whan soules ben broʒt from pyne to blys.</li>
<li>A! how long þey haue þore lyne,</li>
</ul>

who there wait for their Saviour.

<ul style="list-style:none">
<li>To abyde here sauyour yn many a pyne;⁶   772</li>
<li>þey cleped, and cryed, "com goddes sone,</li>
<li>How long shul we yn þys wo wone?"</li>
<li>Here endeþ now crystys passyun,</li>
<li>Fulfylled yn þe oure of syxte and none.   776</li>
</ul>

¹ *t* not quite clear in MS.: *kal* in B.
² *haste* written over in MS.   ³ *shettinge*   ⁴ *heued*
⁵ *mon* follows *deye* in B.   ⁶ *apyne* in MS.

The medytacyun of þe sorowe þat oure Lady had for þe wunde yn here sone[1] syde.

Now gyn we a medytacyun
  Of a swete lamentacyun,
þat mary, modyr meke and mylde,
Made for here derwurþe chylde. 780
Grete peynes she suffred here byfore,
But now she suffreþ moche more;
For whan she say[2] hym drawe to ende,
Y leue she wax oute of here mynde; 784
She swouned, she pyned, she wax half dede,
She fylle to þe grounde, and bette here hede.
þo Ion ran to here, and here vpbreyde.
Whan she myȝt speke, þese wurdes she seyd: 788
"A, my sone! my socour! now wo ys me:
Ho shal graunte me to deye wyþ þe?
þou wrecched deþ, to me þou come,
And do þe modyr dye with þe sone; 792
Aboue alle þyng y desyre þe:
Com deþ, and to my sone þou brynge me.
My fadyr, my former, my mayster, my make,
Why, swete sone, hast þou me forsake? 796
þenk how we loued and leued to gedyr,
And late vs now, dere sone, deye togedyr.
Y may nat lyue here withoute þe,
For alle my fode was þe to se. 800
A sone! where ys now alle my ioyyng,
þat y hadde yn þy furþe beryng?
Y wys þat ioye ys turned to wo:
Symeon seyd soþ hyt shulde be so. 804
He seyd a swerd my soule shulde perce;
Sertes,[3] swete sone, þys y[4] reherce."

A lamentation that Mary made.

She suffered great pains.

She swooned.

788 *She cried,*

"Woe is me!

Come death.

796 [leaf 89, back] *Why, sweet Son, hast thou forsaken me?*

I cannot live without Thee.

The joy I had at Thy birth is turned to woe."

---

[1] sones [2] sagh [3] Certes [4] mai I.

26   MEDITATIONS ON THE

>> "Good women, see if there be any sorrow like unto mine."

>> Never woman bare such a child."

>> An armed company comes to

>> break the legs of the condemned.

>> Mary's martyrdom is renewed.

>> "What more will they do?"

>> I may not help Thee, [leaf 89, bk, col. 2] but I will do what I can."
>> She runs to the cross, and says,

>> "Here will I die."

>> The hounds come,

þan gan here felawshepe here sorowys¹ to aslake,²
And softly and myldely aȝen she þo spake :   808
"Now ȝe gode wymmen, seeþ, with ȝoure yen,
Ȝyf þyr be any sorowe lyke vnto myn :
My sone ys slawe here afore myn ye,
þe whyche y bare wenles³ of my body.   812
þere was neuer womman bare swyche a chylde,
So gode, so gracyus, so meke and so mylde ;
Y feled no sorow yn hys beryng,
Nedys þan mote⁴ yn hys deyyng.   816
Myn owne gete⁵ ys fro me take,
What wundyr ys þan þoȝ y wo make ?"
Whyles she sate yn here lamentacyun,
A cumpany armed she say⁶ fast come ;   820
þe whych ware sent yn a grete reke,⁷
þe dampned mennes legges to breke ;
To sley hem and kast here bodyes away,
þat none shulde se hem hange yn þe halyday.   824
A, mary, modyr, þy wo wexyþ newe !
Se, man, here martyrdom, and þeron rewe.
For so oft she was martyred to day,
As ofte as here sone turmented she say.   828
She seyd, "my sone, what wul⁸ þey more do,
Haue þey nat crucyfyed and slayn þe þerto ?
Y wende þey had be all ful of þe.
Now derwurþe sone, haue reuþe on me.   832
Sone, y may helpe þe yn no degre,
But ȝyt wyl y do þat ys yn me."
To þe cros foote hastly she ran,
And clypped þe cros faste yn here arme,   836
And seyd, "my sone here wyl y dey,
Ar þou from⁹ me be bore aweye."
Faste þese houndes come rennyng ryue,¹⁰
And founde þe Iewes boþe alyue ;   840

¹ sorowe   ² slake   ³ wēles   ⁴ mote I.   ⁵ gete sone
⁶ sngh   ⁷ Glossed *haste* in B.   ⁸ mowe   ⁹ fro   ¹⁰ riue

Þey brak here þyes boþe atwynne,
And founde a grete dyche and kast hem þer ynne.
Se¹ wende þey wulde so serue here sone,
And poȝt with mekenes hem ouercome ; 844
On knees she knelyd with here felawshepe,
And seyd, "seres, y prey ȝow of frenshepe,
Pyneþ² hym no more, brekeþ nat hys þees ;³
Ȝyueþ hym me hole,⁴ for ded ȝe ⁵seeþ he⁶ ys ; 848
Y wyl hym byrye my self and ouþer,
Haueþ reuþe on me, hys sory modyr."
Ey, lady ! what do ȝe to knele wepyng
þus at þese houndes fete, socour⁶ sekyng ? 852
Of salamons sawys ȝe are nat auysed,
þat meknes of proude men ys alle dyspysed.
Þan longeus þe knyȝt dyspysed here pleynt,
þat þo proude was, but now, be⁷ mercy, a seynt. 856
A spere he sette to crystys syde,
He launced and opun[de]⁸ a wounde ful wyde.
Þurgh⁹ hys herte he prened hym with mode,
And anone ran downe watyr¹⁰ and blode. 860
AA,¹¹ wrong ! aa, wo ! aa, wykkednes !
To martyre here¹² for here mekenes.
Þe sone was dede he felte no smerte,
But certes hyt perced þe modrys hert. 864
Þey wounded here, and heped harm vp on harmes ;
She fyl, as for dede, yn maudeleyns armys.
A ! Ihesu, þys dede ys wundyr to me,
þat þou suffrest þy modyr be martyred for þe. 868
Þo Ion stert vp fresshly a none,
And seyd, "wykked men, what wul ȝe done ?
Haue ȝe nat slayn hym with wrong and wo ?
What wyl ȝe sle hys modyr also ? 872
Goþ hens, for we wyl byrye hym anone."

¹ She ² Peineþ ³ þes ⁴ hool ⁵⁻⁵ seþ his ⁶ secour
⁷ bi ⁸ de illegible in MS. ; openede B. ⁹ Thurgh-out
¹⁰ boþe water ¹¹ Au ¹² his moder

Side notes: and break the thieves' legs and cast their bodies into a ditch. Mary kneels before them and says, "Sirs, you see He is dead. I will bury Him. Have pity on me." Ecclus. xiii. 20. Longinus pierces His side with a spear. What wrong, to martyr her for her meekness! She falls for dead into Magdalen's arms. John cries, "Go hence, wicked men, [leaf 00] we will bury Him."

MEDITATIONS ON THE

They go away ashamed.
Al ashamed þe houndes awey gun[1] gone.
Whan mary was waked oute of here swoun,
Aȝens þe cros she sate[2] here adowne; 876
Pytusly she behelde þat grysly wounde;
Fro wepyng she ne myȝt stynte[3] no stounde.

What sorrow they all made no tongue can tell.
What sorowe made Ione, crystys derlyng,
What maudeleyn, with teres hys fete wasshyng, 880
What Iacobe, what cleophe, and ouþer mo,
Y wys no tunge may telle here wo.

Ful feyn þey wulde Ihesu down taken,

They cannot take the Body down.
But strengþe and ynstrumentys boþe þey lakkyn. 884
Among hem þey kast þe best to done,
Sum seyd þe nyȝt wulde nyghe ful sone:
Ȝyf we here wake, deþ shul we þole,[4]
Ȝyf we go hens,[5] þys body shal be stole. 888

They pray to God,
þey preyde to god sum socur hem sende,
For lyfe ne for deþ þey nolde þens[6] wende.

and then see men approaching with instruments.
A newe cumpanye þey say þo comyngge,
Instrumentys and oynementys with hem bryngyngge.
Oure lady dred sore þat þey were enmyes, 893
Tyl Ihone on hem hadde sette gode aspyes;

John recognizes Joseph of Arimathea and Nicodemus.
"Beþe of gode cumforte," he seyde, "þey seme
Ioseph of barmathy and nychodeme." 896
þys was here comyng; whan þey come þedyr

They worship the cross.
þey wurscheped þe cros and salude to gedyr,
And þanked god þat þedyr hem sente:
Oure lady preyd hem to[7] do here entent. 900

The medytacyun of þe oure of euensong.

Now wyl y telle of euensong oure.
Se, man, a syȝte of grete doloure:

Two ladders stand before the cross. Joseph and Nicodemus go up with pincers
Twey laddres afore[8] þe cros now stonde,
Ioseph and nychodeme to clymbe þey fonde, 904
With pynsours, pryuyly, and ouþer gere.

[1] þan gun   [2] sette   [3] stente   [4] B has the gloss *suffre*.
[5] hennes   [6] þennes   [7] *om*.   [8] before

Whan þey to þe hondes come were,
Pryuyly with here pynsours sore þey plyȝt,
Lest marye shulde gryse sore of þat syȝte. 908 to draw out the nails.
þey haled harde ar hyt wulde be, [leaf 90, col. 2]
þe nayles stokyn so fast yn þe tre;
Ful faste þey wrastyn, no þyng þey wounden,
Nedes þey mote¹ brese foule hys houden; 912 They bruise His hands,
But ryȝtwus god acceptþ alle þyng but God accepts a man according to
Of eche man, mekely aftyr hys menyng. his meaning.
Whan þey hadde drawe oute þe nayles with fors,
Ioseph bare vp þe precyous cors, 916
Whyl hys felawe to þe fete wente,
And myȝtily þat nayle oute he hente.
Whan þe nayles were oute echone,
Nychodeme pryuyly toke hem to Ione. 920 The nails are given to John.
Anone runne to alle þat ² were þere,² All help to carry the Body.
And hylpe þat precyus body to bere. John bears the breast,
Ion bare hys breste and wepte ful sore,
For þeron he rested þe nyȝt before; 924
Hys fete bare maudeleyn and on hem weep, Magdalen the feet,
For at hem here synnes she lette;³
þo þat were þere bare alle þe touþer,
Saue hys ryȝt honde bare marye hys modyr. 928 Mary His right hand.
Feyn wulde she ha bore more of here dere sone,
But grete sorowe here strengþe had ouercome.
þat arme wepyng ofte⁴ she kyste, She kisses it,
She kolled hyt, she⁵ clypped hyt vp on here brest. 932
But euer whan she behelde þat grysly wounde,
For sorowe & for feyntnes she fyl to þe grounde.
Oftyn she seyd, "a, sone! a,⁶ sone! and cries,
Where ys now alle þat werk become, 936 "Ah, Son, where is now Thy work?"
þat þou were wunt to werche with þys honde,
Feuers and syke men to brynge oute of bonde?
A, flesshe! a, fode! moste feyre and most fre,

¹ moten ²⁻² þere were ³ leet ⁴ ful ofte
⁵ and ⁶ om.

30 MEDITATIONS ON THE

<table>
<tr><td>Thou hast bought man's sin dear."</td><td></td></tr>
<tr><td>They pray her to hinder them no longer. [leaf 90, back]</td><td></td></tr>
<tr><td>"I pray you," she said, "take Him not from me."</td><td></td></tr>
<tr><td>They prepare to bury Him.</td><td></td></tr>
<tr><td>His Mother sits at the head, and places it in her lap.</td><td></td></tr>
<tr><td>In a story it is said He was shaven;</td><td></td></tr>
<tr><td>the Evangelists say nothing about it.</td><td></td></tr>
<tr><td>Isaiah said,</td><td></td></tr>
<tr><td>My body I gave to the smiters and my cheeks to "men grubbing."</td><td></td></tr>
</table>

Of þe holy goste conceyued yn me, 940
Why fadest þou? no fylþe yn þe ys founde,
For synneles y bare þe yn to þys mounde.
A! mannes synne dere hast þou boȝt,
With a gretter prys myȝt hyt neuer be boȝt." 944
Þys cumpany furþe þan þys cors gun[1] karye,
And prayd[2] hys modyr no lenger hem tarye.
Wyþ oynementys and shetes þey wuldyn hyt dyȝt,
And bery hyt anone for hyt was ny nyȝt. 948
Þan seyd she, "y pray ȝow a bone:
Takeþ nat my sone[3] fro me so[4] sone,
Beryeþ me raþer with hym yn graue,
For, oþer dede or alyue, y mote hym haue." 952
At þe laste she consented,[5] so long þey pray;
Þan to byrye þys body þey hem aray.
Þys body[6] was leyde vpp on a shete,
To anoynte and sewe hyt downe þey sete; 956
Marye hys modyr at þe hede[7] sate;
She lyfte hyt, she leyd hyt feyre yn here lape,
She behylde hyt, how hyt was ybroke,
Prykket, and broysed[8] wyþ many a stroke; 960
Shaue also boþe berde and hede,
With þornes [9]þey rente,[10] with[9] blode alle rede.
Yn a story truly þys resun y nam,
Þat god ones seyd to an holy womman, 964
Whan Iewes had dampned hym deþ for to haue,
Shamely [11]berde and hede[11] gun þey shaue.
The euangelystys telle nat of þys doyng,
For þey myȝte nat wryte alle þyng. 968
Of hys berde y fynde a resun,
Þe whyche seyd[12] Isaye yn goddys persone:
"My body y ȝaue to men smytyng,
And also my chekes to men grubbyng." 972

[1] gun to   [2] preiden   [3] swete sone   [4] þus   [5] consenteþ
[6] body written over in MS.   [7] heued   [8] brissed   [9-9] irent of
[10] for y rente   [11-11] his hede and berde   [12] seiþ

Fyrst, þan, marye, with a swote cloute, — *Mary wrapped His head in a cloth.*
Swaþed here sones hede alle aboute;
"Sone,¹ y was wunt þe swetly to wrappe,
Now swaþe y þe dede, here yn my lappe." 976
The touþer anoynted hym and closed þe shete, — *The others anointed Him.*
Tyl þey com adowne ny to hys fete;
Maudeleyn prayd, þat hys fete sho myȝt² dresse, — *Magdalen prayed to dress His feet.*
For þer she gate of here synnes grace &³ forȝyuenes :
She wepte, and wysshe hem with many a tere, 981 *She washed them with tears.*
She keste hem, and wyped hem with here feyre here.
Whan þe cors alle was ⁴y dyȝt,⁴
To þe sepulcre þey bygan ⁵to bere hyt ful⁵ ryȝt. 984 *They carry Him to the sepulchre,*

The medytacyun of þe oure of cumplyn.

[leaf 90, bk, col. 2]

Now ys þe oure y come of cumplyn :
þey leyn þe cors per⁶ hyt shal lyn, — *and lay Him in it,*
Yn a new sepulcre and feyre y graue,
þat nycodeme made hym self for to haue : 988
þey shette hyt a boute with a grete stone, — *and prepare to leave.*
And arayde hem faste þen for⁷ to gone.
"Abydeþ god breþren, marye gan seye, — *Mary says,*
Wharto hye ȝe so faste aweye? 992 *"Stay: why go so fast?"*
Ȝyf ȝe be ful⁸ of my dere sone,
Goþ hens, and lateþ me here alone wone;
Whedyr shulde y wende, to frende, ouþer kyn? — *Whither should I go?*
Y kan no whedyr go, but ȝyf⁹ y had hym; 996
He was my broþer, my mayster, my spouse;
Now am y¹⁰ wedew, helples yn house. — *Now I am a widow.*
Wuld god ȝe wulde byrye me with hym! — *Would God I were dead.*
For þan shulde we neuer departe¹¹ atwyn. 1000
Now certes my soule ys melted awey :
For ryȝt so¹² loue gan to me seye,

¹ And seide sone ² moste ³ of ⁴⁻⁴ ful weil idight
⁵⁻⁵ hit to bere ⁶ þere-as ⁷ om. ⁸ to ful
⁹ ȝyf written over in MS. ¹⁰ I. a ¹¹ departen
¹² A word partly erased here; apparently *me* or *my*: no word in B.

MEDITATIONS.   4

MEDITATIONS ON THE

<small>I will abide here;</small>
<small>He said He would rise again."</small>
<small>John counsels her to go.</small>
<small>She answers,</small>
<small>"My Son gave me into thy keeping; I must do as thou biddest."</small>
<small>With that she commends her Son to His Father in heaven.</small>
<small>[leaf 91]</small>
<small>"My heart is buried with Thee.</small>
<small>If Thou rise up my heart shall rise also.</small>
<small>If Thou rise not, I am stone dead.</small>
<small>Arise, sweet Son.</small>
<small>Sleep soft in ease;</small>

'Y haue hym soȝt, y fynde hym noȝt,
Y haue hym clepyd, he answereþ noȝt. 1004
Y wyl a byde hym here yn fay,
For he seyde he wulde a ryse þe þryd day.'
But ȝyf þat y hadde trust to hys seyyng,
Myn herte shulde [1]ha broste[1] at hys deyyng." 1008
Þan Ion cunseyled here, and seyd anone,
"Thys sabbat we mow nat wake[2] a lone :
Ȝyf Iewes here vs take þey wyl vs spylle,
And þus was also ȝoure sones wylle." 1012
Þan mary answered, myldely wepyng,
"My sone, Ion, toke me yn þy kepyng,
Y most[3] nedys do as þou me byst : "
And ryȝt with þat wurde aswyþe sho ryst; 1016
Afore þe sepulcre she kneled a downe,
And wepyng, she made þys lamentacyoun :
"A, swete sone ! now wo ys me,
Þat y no lenger may byde with þe, 1020
For nedys y mote now þe forsake,
Þy fadyr of heuene[4] y þe betake ;
Oure felawshepe ys now dyuydyd,
For y may nat with þe be byryed ;[5] 1024
But certes, swete sone, where so euer[6] y be,
Holy myn herte ys byryed with þe ;
Ȝyf þou ryse vp, as þou me behyȝte,
Myn herte shal aryse with þe as lyȝt ; 1028
Ȝyf þou ryse nat vp on þe þrydde day,
Truly y am stonede[7] dede [8]for ay.[8]
Þarfore, swete sone, aryse vp and come,
And kyþe weyl þat þou art of heuene goddys sone."
Þe sepulcre swetly anone she kyst, 1033
Se wente[9] a boute and feyre she hyt blest,
And seyd, "my dere sone, slepe softe yn ese,

<small>[1]–[1] abroste   [2] wake here   [3] mote   [4] final *e* written over in MS.
      [5] iberied   [6] om.   [7] stone
   [8]–[8] for ones *and* al.   eu*er* written above *ay* in MS.
          [9] She romede</small>

For þy place ys made to þe yn pese." 1036   Thy place is in peace.
Eftesones þe sepulcre she kyst knelyng,
And cryde þys wurde with strong wepyng,
"A! sone, here may y no lenger lende,   I may abide no longer.
Nedes from þe þou wylt me sende, 1040
Myn herte with þe y leue to wone,
Farwel, farewel, my derewurþe sone!"   Farewell, my dear Son!"
With þat wurde certes ny swoned she had,
But Ion lefte here vp, and þens¹ here led. 1044   John leads her away.
Towarde þe cyte here wey þey toke,
Oftyn aȝenward marye gan loke.
Whan she come to þe cros, "abydeþ," she seyd;   She stops,
"My sone, my sauyour, ryȝt now here deyd; 1048
Here vpp on he haþ boȝt alle man kynne,
Hys precyus blode haþ wasshe oure synne."
She wurschepyd hyt fyrst, & þan þey echone   and they worship the Cross.
Towarde þe cyte here wey gun they gone. 1052
Are she shulde entre, þey kouerd here vysage.
As for a wedew þey dyd þat vsage.
þey kast where she herbored shulde be,   They "cast" where she should
Eche of hem seyd, "with me, with me." 1056   be lodged. Each says, "With me, with me."
Now þe quene of heuene, modyr hyest,
Haþ nat where yn here hede for to reste.
She þanked hem, and seyd, "y am betake
To Ion, and þarfore y may nat hym forsake." 1060   [leaf 91, col. 2]
Ion seyd, "we wyl with maudeleyn a lyȝt,   John said, "We will stay with Magdalen.
For þere rested oure mayster a whyle to nyȝt;
Also my breþren wyl come alle þedyr;   The brethren will come thither."
þere wyl we reste and speke to gedyr." 1064
þey led here furþe þurgh þat cyte,
Wydewes and wyues of here had pyte.   Widows and wives pity her.
Whan þey had broȝt here þere echone,
Some token here leue and wenten hom; 1068
Maudeleyn and martha were bysy þat nyȝt,
²To serue² here alle þat þey³ myȝt.

¹ þennes   ²—² To ese here and serue   ³ þey written over in MS.

MEDITATIONS ON THE

She could not sleep, but wept and said,
"My dear Son!"

þenke, man, how she myȝt no slepe slepe,
But sorowed, and syghed, and weyled, and wepe, 1072
And euermore seyde, "my derwurþe sone,
For loue y anguysshe tyl þat þou come."

Peter comes weeping, and salutes Mary and John.
The other disciples come,

Anone come petyr, with wepyng chere,
And salude Marye and Ion yn fere. 1076
Þan come þe dyscyplys, eche aftyr oþer,
For shame durst none loke on hys broþer.
Þey asked þe doyng of here dere lorde,

and John tells them all.
"Woe is me," said Peter, "that I forsook Him."

Ion tolde hem þe processe euery aworde. 1080
"Wo me," seyd petyr, "me shameþ to loke,
For þat y my swete lorde and mayster forsoke,
Wheche loued and chersed me[1] so tenderly:
Wo me, a,[2] wreche, mercy, y cry." 1084

The others make their confession and weep.

Also þe dyscyplys here confessyun
Maden and weptyn with[3] lamentacyun.
Þan crystes modyr, here mylde maystres,
Had grete compassyun of here heuynes; 1088

Mary comforts them.

She comforted hem and seyd þus:
"Dysmay ȝow nat for my sone[4] Ihesus,
For þus to hys deþ he wulde be bore,
To saue mannes soule þat was forlore; 1092
Þarto he com with moche stryfe,
Yn traueyle and yn pouert to leden hys lyfe.

"No wonder you forsook Him, His Father did the same."

No wundyr þogh ȝe forsoke hym yn hys ende,
Hys fadyr forsoke hym socour to sende; 1096
Hymself he forsoke for oure mys dede;

[leaf 91, back]

Y preyd for hym, y myȝt no þyng spede;
Certes y am sory for hys grete passyun,
But truly y glade for soules saluacyun; 1100
Þey shulden yn helle for euer be forlore,
But y hym to þys deþ had [5]hym bore;[5]
Ȝe weten weyl how benygne my dere sone was,
Lyȝtly to forȝyue al maner of trespas; 1104

[1] *me* written over in MS.; *mo* follows *louede* in B. [2] aa
[3] wiþ gret [4] swete sone [5–5] here ibore

Douteþ ȝe no þyng of hys grete mercy,
For largely he ȝyfþ þat cryeþ hyt hertly ;
Beeþ of gode cumfort, for trustly y say,   "Be of good comfort;
We shullen hym se on þe þrydde day ;   1108   we shall see Him on the third day."
Seþþen he haþ boght vs at so grete prys,
Nedes from þe deþ he mote aryse."
"Certys," seyd petyr, "þys nyȝt at þe cene,[1]   "Certainly," said Peter,
He seyd eftsones we shuldyn hym sene,   1112   "He said we should soon see Him,
Þan alle oure sorowe to ioye shulde come,   and that our sorrow should be
And þat ioye shulde nat from vs be nome."[2]   turned to joy."
"A ! breþren !" seyd Marye, "y ȝow pray
Þat swete sermoun ȝe wyl me say."   1116
A none Ion tolde here, for he coude best,
For slepyng he soke hyt at crystys brest.
Þus þey dwel yn here medytacyun,   Thus they dwelt until the resurrection.
Tyl tyme was come of þe resurreccyun.   1120

The medytacyun how cryst ȝede to helle.

Thenk, man, and se cryst aftyr hys deþ :
For þy synne streyght to helle he geþ,   For thy sin Christ goeth straight to hell.
Oute of þe fendys bonde to þe fre,
And þe fende bonde to make to þe.   1124
Þenk, also, þe grete dede of hys powere :
He myȝt ha[3] sent an angel to saue vs here,   He might have sent an angel to save us.
But þan of oure saluacyun we shulde nat þanke hym,
But calle þe aungel sauer of alle man kyn.   1128
Þarfor hys fadyr so hertly loued vs,   God so loved us that He gave us His Son.
He ȝaue vs hys owene gete sone Ihesus ;
Þan we onely hym þanke and do hym onoure,
As fadyr, as former, socoure and sauyoure.   1132
Þank we now oure sayoure, þat salue vs haþ broȝt,   Thank we now our Saviour,
Oure syke soules to saue, whan synne haþ hem soȝt.
Of hys grete godenes gyn we hym grete,   [leaf 91, bk, col. 2]
Seyyng þe wurde of sakarye þe holy prophete :   1136   saying the words of Zacharias,

---

[1] Glossed *soper* in B.   [2] Glossed *take* in B.
[3] haue

THE SONG OF ZACHARIAS.

"Blessed be the Lord God of Israel."
S. Luke 1. 68.

"Lorde god of Israel, blessed mote þou be,
þy peple þou hast vysyted and boȝt hem to þe,
Whych setyn yn derkenes of deþ and dysese,
þou lyȝtest hem and ledest yn to þe wey of pese." 1140

To that "peace peerless" bring us. Amen.

To þat pes pereles we prey þou vs bryng,
þat leuyst and reynest with oute endyng. 1142
    Amen.

GLOSSARIAL INDEX.

A, 1084, 1115, ah.
And ther with al he bleynte / and cryde. *A. Chaucer,* 1078.

Adowne, 676, 1017, down.

Afore, 150, 180.

Agadlyng, 477, a gadling, a gadder about; a vagabond. Cp. "They ronne *agaddynge,* ye a whore hountinge after their false prophetes."—*The Lamentacyon of a Christian agaynste the Cyte of London,* leaf 4 (1545).

Al, *Al hole,* 182, all whole, entirely, wholly.

Algate, Algates, 358, 364, 392, 699, always, at all times, under all circumstances; in the last example it means certainly, of a truth, indeed.

Alheyl, 378, All hail!

Al thogh, 56, although.

Alyþed, 589, have allayed, mitigated.

An, 310, 380, 397, on.

Angred, 744, angered, made sorry. "They *angered* Moses also in the tents."—Psa. cvi. 16, *P. B. Vers.*

Anguyssed, 315, pained.

Anguysshe, 1074, to pine, suffer.

Angwys, 659, 683, anguish.

Ar, Are, 31, 94, &c., ere, before.

Aray, 954, 990, to prepare, to make ready.

Areyned, 601, commanded.

Arst, 502, first, formerly.

Aslake, 807, to abate, to slake.

Aspyes, 894, spies.

Astounde, 328.

Astyte, 436, anon, quickly.

Aswyþe, 1016, quickly, immediately.

At, 371, of.

Atwyn, Atwynne, 663, 678, 841, 1000, asunder, "atwo," or in two.

Auysed, 853, informed, taught, advised.

Auysyly, 415, advisedly, carefully.

Awake, 336, arouse.

Aworde, every aworde, 1080, every word.

Axen, 430, ask.

Ay, 1030, ever.

Aysel, 732, vinegar.

Aȝens, 46, 48, "aȝens he com," "aȝens nyȝt," by, just before.

Aȝenward, 1046, backward.

Bacyn, 141, basin.

Bebled, p. 20, *note.*

Behoue, 224, behoof, advantage.
Behynde, 287.
Behyȝte, 1027, promised (compounded of 'be' and 'hight').
Benygne, 1103, benign, kind.
Berdoun, 593, burden.
Betake, 353, 365, 457, 695, 728, 760, bring to, give to, commend to.
Beþ, Beþe, 648, 895, be.
Beþenke, 127, 129, 163, bethink, remember.
Betraye, Betrey, 96, 106, betray.
Bie, p. 2, *note*.
Blyn, 103, to cease, to stop.
Bodly, 39, bodily, corporeal.
Boffeteþ, 428, buffet; *indic. plur.*
Bokes hede, 320, chapter (of a book).
"Brent sacrifise, and for synne thou askidest not; thanne I seide, Lo! I come. In the *hed* of the *boc* it is write of me that I do thi wil."—Psalm xxxix. 8, 9, *Wycliffe's Vers.*
"Thanne I scyde, Loo! I come; in the head, *or bigynnyng*, of the book it is writyn of me."—Heb. x. 7, *Wycliffe's Vers.*
"In capite libri scriptum est de me."—*Vulgate.*
Bollers, 477, drinkers, drunkards, men who pass the bowl. See *P. Plow.*, C-text, Pass. x. 194, and note.
Bone, 313, prayer, petition, request.
Bone, 372, 949, boon, gift.
Bownden, 523, bound.
Breche, 622, breeches, covering.
Brenne, 201, burn.
Brese, 912, bruise.
Broysed, 960, bruised.
But, 666, only, except.
Buxom, 469, obedient.
By, Bye, 28, 318, buy, redeem.

By, "by þe wey," 284.
Byfore, 287.
Byhelde, 489.
Bynte, 427, bind. "The last word *bint* the tale."—Quoted in the *Journ. Sac. Lit.*, vol. i. (1865), p. 252.
Bypaþ, 486, by-path, a secluded way.
Byrye, 849, bury.
Byst, 1015, biddest, requestest.
Byt, 305, bade, warned.

Calle, 1128, call.
Ce to Ce, 441, place to place. Cp. "Cee, Mare, fretum, pontus."—*P. Parv.*, p. 64.
Cene, 1111, Fr. *Cêne*, the Lord's Supper. Sp. *cena*, a supper.
Whan he sat with hem at the *cene*
. . . .
To swych he gaff hem alderlast
Hys owne body.
MS. Cott. Vit. C. xiii., lf 69, bk.
Chalys, 193, chalice.
Chekenes, 286, chickens.
Chere, 11, 87, 1075, cheer, countenance.
Chere, 203, cheering, cheerful.
Chersed, 333, 1083, cherished.
Chese, 393, choose.
Clepe, 719, call.
Cleppeþ, 152, clippeth, embraceth.
Cleuyn, 616, ? clewe, fasten on, seize.
Cloute, 973, cloth.
Clypped, 932, embraced, pressed closely.
Compyled, 14, compiled.
Comunde, 198, communed, conversed with.
Conceyued, 910, conceived.
Constreyned, 602, constrained, compelled.

GLOSSARIAL INDEX. 39

Cors, 916, 945, corse, a dead body.
Corupt, 27, corrupt.
Coude, 126, could.
Croys, 556, cross.
Crucyfyers, 642.
Cryeþ, 1106, asketh, demandeth.
Crysten, 9, christian, christened.
Cumplyn, 985, even-song, the last service of the day; compline.
Cumþ, 418, cometh.

Dame, 286, mother's.
Dampne, 556, 558, 559, condemn.
Day, 728, die.
Defoule, 506, defile, pollute.
Degre, 7, degree, condition in life.
Deluyn, 347, dig, delve.
Derkenes, 1139, darkness.
Derlyng, 276, dearling, darling.
Derwurly, 180, cheerfully, willingly, honourably.
þe sculen biwiten þene king! durewurþliche þurh alle þing.
Laȝamons Brut., ii. 210.
þise were diȝt on þe des, & derwarþly scrued.
Sir Gawayne, 114.
Derwurþ, Derwurþe, 181, 368, 385, 651, precious, very dear.
Deye, 94, 207, die.
Do, 131, "was do," was done.
Done, wuld done, 138.
Dresse, 158, prepare.
Drye, 738, dry, thirsty. "Dry fro moysture. *Siccus.*"—*P. Parv.*
Dung, 506.
Dyffyed, 743, defied, rejected, despised. "*Dyffyyn*, or vtterly dyspysyn. *Vilipendo, floccipendo, sperno, aspernor, aporio.*"—*P. Parv.* 115.
Dyggen, 611, dig.
Dyrknes, 410, darkness.

Dysese, 1139, disease, trouble.
Dyspetusly, 615, angrily, without pity.
Dysplayed, 640, displayed, extended, spread out.
Dyspoyle, 615, despoil, spoil, undress.
Dysturbled, 316, disturbed, troubled. "*Dysturbelyn, Turbo, conturbo.*"—*P. Parv.* 123.
"And thei . . . . weren *distourblid*, seyinge, For it is a fantum.*"—S. Matt. xiv. 26. "He began for to be *distourblid* and sory in herte."—S. Matt. xxvi. 37, *Wycliffe*.
Dyȝt, 49, 325, prepared, made ready.

Echone, 57, all, each one.
Eftesones, Eftsones, 549, 1037, 1112, immediately.
Eke, 506, also.
Enformed, 238, informed, taught.
Entent, 43, "Take gode entent," give good heed.
Erst, 424, before, formerly: *arst* in l. 502.
Ese, 1035, ease, rest.
Euerychone, 132, every one.
Expouñed, 735, expounded, explained.
Ey, 851, eh?

Fare, 492, suffer, endure.
Fay, 1005, faith, confidence.
Fedyng, 35, 39, feeding.
Felawshepe, 447, 576, company, companions.
Fele, 669, many.
Fere, 68, 88, 119, 240. In fere, together, in company, one with another; l. 240, "loue yn fere," love one another. "This is my

GLOSSARIAL INDEX.

comaundement, that ȝe loue to gidere."—S. John xv. 12, *Wycliffe*.
Fere, 580, a companion.
Fersly, 626, fiercely.
Fest, 212, fist, hand.
Fette, fet, 82, 563, 614, fetched.
Feye, 18, 86, faith, belief.
Feyn, 686, fain, gladly, willingly.
Feynt, 509, faint, weak.
Feyntly, 572, faintly, weakly.
Feyntnesse, 594.
Feyre, 164, 169. In l. 164 the Lat. orig. has *five*.
Feyre, 1034, fair.
Folue, 177, follow.
Fond, 356, found.
Fonde, 187, founded, instituted.
Fong, 329, to endure, suffer.
For, 273, because.
Fordone, 186, destroy, do away with. *Fordone* is properly the participle of *for-do*.
Forlore, 26, utterly lost.
Former, 795, Maker, Creator.
Forwounded, 519, much wounded.
Fresshly, 869, fiercely, briskly.
Furþe, 802, "furþe beryng," birth, bringing forth.
Fyne, 656, perfectly, quite.
Fynst, 557, findest.
Fyrþer more, 621.
Fyþe, 729, fifth.
Fyueþe, 257, fifth.

Gan, 185, began.
Gere, 657, 905, gear, tools.
Gert, 139, girded, girt.
Gerte, 654, pushed, drove.
Gete, 817, 1130, gotten, begotten.
Geþ, 1122, goeth.

Gladlygh, 89, gladly, cheerfully.
Glymbe, 630, climb.
Gobbettes, 85, morsels, bits.
Gone, 1052, "gan gone," began to go.
Graces, 81, prayers before meat.
Grame, 548, to anger.
Graue, y graue, 987, dug.
Grete, 1135, greet, address.
Greyþe, 46, prepare, make ready.
Grubbyng, 972. In Wycliffe's translation this passage (Isa. l. 6) stands thus: "My bodi I ȝaf to the smyteres, and my chekes to the pulleris; my face I turnede not awei fro the blameres, and the spitteres in me."
Gryse, 153.
Grysly, 101, sorrowful.
Grysly, 877, 933, terrible, frightful.
Gun, 630, 945, 966, gan, began.
Gunne, 133, began.
Gyn, 777, 1135, begin.

Ha, 686, 929, 1126, have.
"He wolde *ha* men · as lord to hym loute."
See *Gospel Stories, Man who made a Supper* (p. 6).
Haled, 662, pulled.
Halfdede, 588, half dead.
Hardy, 526.
He, 254.
Hem, 259, "hem whyche."
Hen, 280, hence.
Hente, 918, drew.
Hepys, 624, hips.
Herbored, 1055, lodged.
Herdles, 452, herdless, without a shepherd.
Here, 63, their.
Here by, 67.

GLOSSARIAL INDEX.

Hertly, 243, 1106, heartily.
Hestes, hestys, 323, 742, commands, behests.
Ho, 528, 790, who.
Ho, 573, he.
Hole, 182, "al hole," wholly, entirely.
Holy, 1026, wholly.
Hom, 1068.
Homely, 275. Will the reader supply a word which will convey the sense as well as this does?
Hote, 240, command.
Hyde, 623, hye, 573, hyed, 590, hyyng, 627, to hurry, hurried, hurrying.
Hylpe, 922, helped, assisted.
Hyt, 102, it.

Instrumentys, 892, instruments.
Ioed, 562, joyed.
Iuwyse, 577, I-wis.

Kast, 643, lifted, raised.
Kast, 885, 1055, cast, considered.
Kercheues, 624, kerchiefs.
Knowlechyng, 424, knowledge.
Kolled, 932, embraced, clasped.
Kone, 438, can.
Kouerd, 1053, covered.
Kraked, 662, cracked, broke.
Krokedly, 571, crookedly.
Krokyng, 149, crooking, bending.
Kunne, 675, can.
Kynne, 1049, man kynne, mankind.
Kyþe, 1032, know.
Kytte, 85, 236, 268, cut, pierced. It *kittiþ myn herte as with a knyf*. *Pol., Rel., and Love Poems*, p. 205, l. 16.
Lake, 347, a pit.

Lakkyn, 884, lack.
Lamaȝabatany, 724. See St Matt. xxvii. 46.
Lape, 958, lap.
Lateþ, 467, 994, let, allow, permit.
Launced, 858, lanced, pierced with a lance.
Lede, 665, ? lead, the metal.
Lemes, 667, limbs.
Lende, 1039, remain, tarry.
Lere, 13, 16, 67, 120, learn.
Lered, 170, learned.
Lese, 394, lose.
Lestene, 312, listen.
Lete, 165, 181, } left, ? leave.
Lette, 926,
Leue, 784, believe.
Lewed, 170, ignorant.
Leyd, 274, " be leyd," laid low, overcome.
Leyn, 521, "leyn on," lay on, thrash.
Leyn, 986, lay.
Logher, 133, lower.
Loke, 167, see, behold.
Lone, 1010, "a lone," alone.
Lore, 673, learning, knowledge, doctrine.
Louesum, 220, lovely, loving.
Lyn, 986, lie, remain.
Lyne, 733, slake, stop.
Lyne, 771, lain, remained.
Lys, 702, ease, relieve, lessen.
Lyȝt, 1061, "a lyȝt," remain, stay.
Lyȝt, 47, remained, tarried.
Lyȝt, 207, alighted, came down.
Lyȝtly, 1104, willingly, quickly, commonly.

Make, 795, mate, companion, equal.

GLOSSARIAL INDEX.

Manly, 398, manfully.
Many one, 541.
Mede, 335, value, worth.
Mekest, 645, humblest (verb).
Memorand, 32, memorable.
Memorand, 195, a memorial.
Mende, 127, mind.
Mende, 196, memory.
Mercyable, 456, mercyful.
Mest, 400, most.
Meyny, 198, company.
Mode, 345, 859, wrath, anger.
Monasshyng, 169, 245, admonishing, admonition.
Mone, 454, moan, supplication.
Mone, 715, told, said, made. Qy. moaned? But B. has *nome*, took.
Moste, 199, 528.
Mot, Mote, 390, 581, must.
Mounde, 942, the earth, the world.
Mow, 349, 350, 363, may.
Mow, 522, might, could, were able (to do).
Mysdo, 462, misdone, done amiss.
Mysdoer, 503, a wrong-doer.
Myþe, 156, mighty. See *myhthy* in Prompt. Parv. (? *mild*.)

Nam, 603, 963, took.
Nat, 590, not.
Nayles, 116, nails.
Neme, 513, "vndyr neme," ? examine, punish.
Ner, 586, nearer.
Nolde, 890, ne would, would not.
Nome, 1114, taken.
Noþer, 27, neither.
Noye, 22, annoy.
Noȝt, 22, "with noȝt," in any manner, in anything.

Ny, 418, nigh, near.
Nygh, 90, nigh, near.
Nyghe, 886, come, approach.

O, 68, 382, one.
Ones, 964, once.
Onoure, 1131, honour.
Opone, 10, open.
Opunly, 543, openly.
Opynyons, 20, opinions.
Orcherd, 303, orchard, garden.
Orysun, 361, orison.
Oute, 615; "*oute* dyspetusly," without pity.
Owne, 817, 1130, "owne gete," only begotten.
Oynementys, 892, 947, ointments.

Pas, 359, "toke hys pas," went his way.
Paske, 82, paschal.
Paske, 94, passover.
Pens, 335, pence.
Pereles, 1141, peerless.
Pese, 1036, 1140, peace, rest.
Pleynes, 689, complains.
Pleynt, 510, plaint, complaint, indictment.
Plogh, 568, plough.
Plyȝt, 626, plucked, taken away.
Plyȝt, 907, pulled.
Pouert, 1094, poverty.
Prened, 859, pierced, pricked.
Preued, 18, proved.
Preyour, 413.
Preysed, 336, appraised, valued.
Processe, 1080, the manner in which an act was done; details, particulars.
Pryme, 475, 537, prime; six o'clock in the morning.

GLOSSARIAL INDEX. 43

Pryncypals, 226, heads of a discourse.
Pryuyly, 105, privily, secretly.
Punged, 567, pricked, goaded.
Pur, 8, for.
Put, 141.
Pycchen, 612, pitch, throw, or let fall.
Pyler, pylour, 523, 515, pillar.
Pyne, 401, 547, pain, grief.
Pyneþ, 847, punish, torture, *imperat. plur. 2nd pers.*
Pynsours, 905, pincers.
Pytusly, 533, grievously. Cp. "*Pytyows*, or rufulle yn syʒhte. *Dolorosue, penosus.*"—*P. Parv.* 402.
Real, 33, 34.
Reke, 821, hurry, haste.
Rent (verb), 116, rend.
Reuþe, 832, 850, pity, compassion.
Rewe, 473, 826, to regret, be sorry for: to rue.
Reyʒte, 642, raught, reached.
Riue, note to l. 839.
Route, 423, a company.
Ruly, 121, 301, 517, 634, rueful. "*Ruly, idem quod* ruful (ful of ruthe and pyte)."—*P. Parv.* 439.
Ryme, 538 (verb).
Ryst, 1016, arose.
Ryue, 839.
Ryʒtwus, 913, righteous.
Salude, 898, 1076, saluted.
Salue, 1133, salve, salvation.
Samen, 671, "yn samen," in company, together.
Sauer, 1128, saver, Saviour.
Sawys, "Salamons sawys," sayings, proverbs.
  Sum *sawes* of Sulomon · y shall you shew sone.
    The Crowned King, l. 44.

The passage is, "As the proud hate humility: so doth the rich abhor the poor."—Ecclus. xiii. 20.
Say, 587, 688, saw.
Scorneþ, scorned, 429, 743.
Se, 843, 1034, she.
Seced, 100, ceased.
Seche, 621, ? to look, to observe.
Secundo, 40, second.
Seluyn, 453, "here seluyn," herself; owne self, 680.
Semely, 387, properly, becomingly, justly.
Sen, 232, see (1*st pers. indic. fut.*).
Setyn, 1139, sit.
Sewe, 402, ensue, follow.
Sewe, 956, to sew.
Sey, 134, seen.
Seyn, seyd, 134, 553, say, said.
Seyth, "sum seyth," 675.
Seyyng, 228, saying.
Shamely, 966, shamefully.
Shape, 575, "hym ys shape," for him is prepared, or intended; devised.
Shaue, 966, shave; 961, shaven.
Shenshepe, 448, 575, punishment.
Shete, 955, Shetes, 947, sheet, sheets.
Shokyn, 479, shook.
Shulder, 565, shoulder.
Shullen, 1108, shall.
Shust, 714, shouldest.
Shyttyng, 756, shutting.
Slake, 696, mitigate.
Slogh, 567, slough, a dirty place.
Smert, 140, smart, quick, quickly.
Soper, 30, 33, supper.
Sopyng place, 160, supping place.
Speʊyal, 107, special.
Spelle, 114, learn, read.

GLOSSARIAL INDEX.

Spelle, 130, teach.
Spelled, 739, uttered, said.
Sprunge, 414, "be sprunge," besprinkled.
Spyl, spylle, spylled, 470, 582, 600, 752, 1011, spoil, destroy, punish.
Stant, 681, stands.
State, 391, manner.
Stede, 135, place.
Sterte, 421, hurried, went forward.
Sterte, 570, "a sterte," start away, turn away, wander.
Steuene, 382, voice.
Stey, 635, "vpp stey," raised, elevated.
Stilly, 689, softly, silently.
Stokyn, 910, stuck.
Stonede dede, 1030, "stone dead."
Stonen, 141, of stone, of earthenware.
Story, 963, history, legend.
Stounde, 878, a moment, a short space of time.
Straked, 661, proceeded, went.
Streyght to helle, 1122.
Strey3te, 641, stretched.
Stye, 208, to ascend.
Stynte, 878, stint, stop, cease.
Sum, 684, somewhat, partly.
Sumdele, 702, 733, somewhat, a little.
Sustryn, 647, sisters.
Swaþe, 974, 976, wrap.
Swote, 370, 379, sweat.
Swouned, 785, swooned.
Swyche, 508, 813, such.
Swyþe, 137, "swyþe sone," very soon. See *Aswyþe.*
Syghyng, 271.

Syre, 501, 535, sire, sir.
Syxte, 606.

Tagh, 243, 279, taught.
Tary, 560, 597, tarry, delay.
Tendyrly, 119, tenderly.
Teren, 634, tears.
Teþ, 116, teeth.
þe, 69, they.
þees, 847, thighs.
þeke, 446, that.
þeron, 924.
þeuys, 576, thieves.
þo, 98, 423, 432, then, at that time.
Thogh, 104, "as þogh," though.
þole, 887, suffer.
þore, 757, there.
þred, 41, 538, third.
þrest, 289, thrust.
þryd, þrydde, 179, 245, third.
þryst, 733, thirst.
þrysted, 736, desired.
þrysted, 737, thirsted.
þrytty, 335, thirty.
þryys, 360, thrice.
þurgh, 623, 859, through.
þyes, 841, thighs.
Thyr, 22, there.
þyrwhylys, 367, 443, therewhiles, during that time.
To, 362, two, or twice.
To braste, 566.
Toke, 168, 278, 1014, gave.
Too, 654, two.
Toure, 376, tower.
Touþer, 656.
Tray, 156, betray.
Trewe, 58, true, faithful.
Trustly, 1107, confidently, truly.

Trusty, 58, trustworthy.
Tugge, 441, pull violently.
Twey, 50, 629, two.
Twyys, 360.

Varye, 598, alter, change.
Ver, 583, "a ver," afar, at a distance.
Verry, 84, true, real.
Vnder neme, 513, ? examine.
Vnsekernes, 440.
Vpbreyde, 787.
Vsage, 1054.
Vyleynsly, 580, villanously.
Vysage, 1053, visage, face.

Wadeþ, 520, wades.
Wake, 305, 358, 887, watch.
Wax, 369, 784, grew.
Wenles, 812, wemless, spotless.
Werche, 937, to work, perform.
Werchyng, 200, deed, undertaking.
Weren, 633, were.
Wete, 506, wet, water.
Weten, 1103, know.
Weyle, 450, wail.
Wharto, 725, whereto, for what purpose.
Whet, 631, whetted, pointed.
Whyle, 1062, "a whyle," a-while, for a time.
Witnesseþ, 51, bears witness.
Wode, 617, mad.
Wo me, 1081.
Wone, 262, dwelling place, world.
Wone, 750, to dwell.

Wrake, 366, 458, destruction, mischief, harm.
Wrappe, 975.
Wrastyn, 911, wrest, strain, pull.
Wraþþe, 345, (glossed) wrath.
Wroþer, 290 (a comparative), more angry.
Wryde, 624, wrapped, covered.
Wul, 829, would, will.
Wuld, "wuld God," 999.
Wuldyn, 947, would (*plur.*).
Wunt, 937, 975, wont, in the habit of (doing).
Wykked, 870.
Wynne, 6, gain, obtain, win.
Wyse, 144, "alle wyse."
Wysshe, 166, washed.
Wyte, 339, wete, knew.

Y, 102, I.
Y, 500, in.
Y, 120, 882, "y wys," I-wis, truly, certainly.
Ye, *plur.* yen, 101, 357, 643, eye.
Ylad, 487, led.
Ynstrumentys, 884, instruments.

ȝede, went, p. 35.
ȝenseyyng, 637, opposition, strife, gainsaying.
ȝoue, 331, given, rewarded.
ȝow, 314, thee.
ȝulde, 346, given, rewarded.
ȝungeste, 56, youngest.
ȝyfte, 181, gift.
ȝyfþ, 1106, giveth.
ȝyueþ, 848.

The manufacturer's authorised representative in the EU for product safety is Oxford University Press España S.A. of El Parque Empresarial San Fernando de Henares, Avenida de Castilla, 2 - 28830 Madrid (www.oup.es/en or product.safety@oup.com). OUP España S.A. also acts as importer into Spain of products made by the manufacturer.

Printed and bound by CPI Group (UK) Ltd, Croydon, CR0 4YY

23/03/2026

02076308-0002